Green Egg Extravaganza: 101 Recipes for Grilling and Smoking with the Big Green Egg

Hot Dog Stand Tera

Copyright © 2023 Hot Dog Stand Tera
All rights reserved.
:

Contents

INTRODUCTION 7
1. Grilled Steak with Chimichurri Sauce 8
2. Smoked Pork Ribs with Barbecue Sauce 9
3. Grilled Chicken Skewers with Lemon Herb Marinade 9
4. Smoked Brisket with Homemade Rub 10
5. Grilled Salmon with Dill Sauce 11
6. Smoked Turkey Breast with Cranberry Glaze 12
7. Grilled Shrimp Tacos with Avocado Salsa 13
8. Smoked Pulled Pork Sandwiches with Coleslaw 14
9. Grilled Lamb Chops with Mint Pesto 15
10. Smoked Sausages with Mustard Sauce 16
11. Grilled Vegetables with Balsamic Glaze 17
12. Smoked Chicken Wings with Spicy Buffalo Sauce 18
13. Grilled Portobello Mushrooms with Balsamic Reduction 19
14. Smoked Beef Tenderloin with Horseradish Cream 20
15. Grilled Mahi Mahi with Mango Salsa 21
16. Smoked Baby Back Ribs with Honey Glaze 22
17. Grilled Teriyaki Chicken Skewers 23
18. Smoked Pork Belly Burnt Ends 24
19. Grilled Vegetable Kabobs with Herb Marinade 24
20. Smoked Salmon with Lemon Dill Butter 26
21. Grilled Ribeye Steak with Herb Butter 26
22. Smoked Chicken Thighs with BBQ Dry Rub 27
23. Grilled Swordfish with Lemon Caper Sauce 28
24. Smoked Bratwurst with Beer Braised Onions 29
25. Grilled Asparagus with Parmesan Cheese 30
26. Smoked Beef Ribs with Espresso BBQ Sauce 31
27. Grilled Shrimp Scampi with Garlic Butter 32

28. Smoked Duck Breast with Orange Glaze 33

29. Grilled Zucchini with Feta and Mint 34

30. Smoked St Louis Style Ribs with Sweet and Spicy Rub 35

31. Grilled Chicken Caesar Salad 36

32. Smoked Pork Shoulder with Carolina BBQ Sauce 37

33. Grilled Pineapple with Brown Sugar Glaze 38

34. Smoked Lamb Racks with Rosemary Garlic Marinade 39

35. Grilled Halloumi Skewers with Lemon Herb Dressing 40

36. Smoked Corned Beef with Mustard Glaze 40

37. Grilled Eggplant with Tahini Sauce 41

38. Smoked Sausage and Peppers 42

39. Grilled Tandoori Chicken with Yogurt Marinade 43

40. Smoked Prime Rib with Herb Crust 44

41. Grilled Watermelon Salad with Feta and Mint 45

42. Smoked Chicken Drumsticks with Spicy Rub 46

43. Grilled Scallops with Lemon Butter Sauce 47

44. Smoked Pork Tenderloin with Apple Chutney 48

45. Grilled Sweet Potato Wedges with Chipotle Mayo 49

46. Smoked Beef Brisket Burnt Ends 50

47. Grilled Caesar Salad with Grilled Chicken 51

48. Smoked Tri-Tip with Chimichurri Sauce 52

49. Grilled Peaches with Honey Mascarpone 53

50. Smoked Turkey Legs with Maple Glaze 54

51. Grilled Halloumi Salad with Lemon Vinaigrette 55

52. Smoked Salmon Crostini with Herbed Cream Cheese 56

53. Grilled T-Bone Steak with Garlic Herb Butter 57

54. Smoked Pork Chops with Apple Bourbon Glaze 57

55. Grilled Vegetable Platter with Dips 58

56. Smoked Meatloaf with BBQ Sauce 60

57. Grilled Octopus with Lemon Garlic Sauce 61
58. Smoked Chicken and Sausage Jambalaya 61
59. Grilled Halloumi Skewers with Mediterranean Salsa 63
60. Smoked Stuffed Bell Peppers 64
61. Grilled Lemon Herb Chicken Wings 65
62. Smoked Beef Short Ribs with Red Wine Glaze 66
63. Grilled Shrimp and Pineapple Skewers with Teriyaki Glaze 67
64. Smoked Lamb Burgers with Tzatziki Sauce 68
65. Grilled Zucchini Rolls with Goat Cheese and Sun-Dried Tomatoes 69
66. Smoked Chicken Fajitas with Peppers and Onions 69
67. Grilled Steak Fajitas with Salsa and Guacamole 70
68. Smoked Pork Loin with Apple Cider Glaze 71
69. Grilled Halloumi Burger with Roasted Red Pepper Sauce 72
70. Smoked Stuffed Mushrooms with Cream Cheese and Bacon 74
71. Grilled Herb-Marinated Tofu Skewers 74
72. Smoked Cornish Hens with Herb Butter 75
73. Grilled Teriyaki Salmon with Sesame Seeds 77
74. Smoked Meatballs with Tangy BBQ Sauce 77
75. Grilled Shrimp Po' Boy Sandwiches with Remoulade Sauce 78
76. Smoked Chicken Enchiladas with Green Chile Sauce 80
77. Grilled Artichokes with Lemon Garlic Aioli 81
78. Smoked Beef Kabobs with Garlic Herb Marinade 82
79. Grilled Portobello Burger with Avocado and Pesto 83
80. Smoked Turkey Burgers with Cranberry Mayo 84
81. Grilled Veggie Quesadillas with Guacamole 85
82. Smoked Stuffed Jalapeños with Cream Cheese and Bacon 86
83. Grilled Lemon Herb Swordfish Steaks 86
84. Smoked Baby Back Ribs with Coffee Rub 87

85. Grilled Chicken Satay Skewers with Peanut Sauce 88
86. Smoked Pork Chops with Maple Dijon Glaze 89
87. Grilled Halloumi and Watermelon Skewers......................................90
88. Smoked Bratwurst with Sauerkraut and Mustard............................91
89. Grilled Sweet and Spicy Chicken Wings..92
90. Smoked Tri-Tip Sandwiches with Horseradish Sauce....................93
91. Grilled Vegetable Pasta Salad with Pesto Dressing 94
92. Smoked Chicken Sausage with Peppers and Onions......................95
93. Grilled Balsamic Glazed Brussels Sprouts 96
94. Smoked Salmon Dip with Dill and Cream Cheese 97
95. Grilled Tandoori Shrimp Skewers 98
96. Smoked Pork Belly with Honey Soy Glaze......................................99
97. Grilled Portobello Mushroom Burger with Balsamic Reduction 100
98. Smoked Beef Tenderloin with Blue Cheese Butter 101
99. Grilled Pineapple Upside-Down Cake..102
100. Smoked Apple Crisp with Vanilla Ice Cream 102
101. Grilled Banana Splits with Chocolate Sauce................................103
CONCLUSION 105

INTRODUCTION

Welcome to the Green Egg Extravaganza! This cookbook is a celebration of different recipes you can make with the Big Green Egg. In this book, you will find delicious, creative, and traditional recipes, as well as recipes with exciting new flavor profiles and combinations. With 101 recipes, you can easily find something to fit the most discerning palates.

Each recipe is composed of fresh, health-conscious ingredients, perfect for the everyday home chef. Whether you are a novice cook or a seasoned professional, you will find something here that will make all your meals more flavorful. From slow-cooked barbeque to smoky grilled meats, there is something delicious for everyone.

To get the best flavor out of your Big Green Egg, you will need to hone your skills in grilling and smoking. With the help of this cookbook, you will be able to gain the confidence and expertise necessary to live up to its reputation as the world's finest smoker and outdoor cooker. From roasting to baking, this cookbook has you covered for every delicious variety of food that the Big Green Egg can offer you—it's time to get grilling!

The Big Green Egg is a unique ceramic cooker that allows you to flawlessly recreate your favorite grilled dishes and discover new flavors. Its versatility ensures that you can create an endless variety of dishes perfect for any occasion. With minimal clean-up and easy to use features, even the novice cook can grill like a pro.

So, it's time to say goodbye to the boring and bland, and start your journey into a world of vibrant and flavorful main courses, sides, and desserts. Get ready for a Green Egg Extravaganza! With 101 recipes, you can find something for every palate and celebrate the wonderful flavors that the Big Green Egg brings. Let the grilling and smoking begin!

1. Grilled Steak with Chimichurri Sauce

Grilled Steak with Chimichurri Sauce is a delicious and flavorful dinner entrée that is sure to be a hit with the whole family. With steak, garlic, and fresh herbs, it's a dish you won't soon forget.
Serving: 4 Servings
Preparation time: 10 minutes
Ready time: 15 minutes

Ingredients:
- 4 steaks of your choice
- 2 cloves of garlic, minced
- 1/2 cup olive oil
- 2 tablespoons red wine vinegar
- 1/4 cup fresh parsley, chopped
- 2 tablespoons fresh oregano, chopped
- 1 tablespoon freshly squeezed lemon juice
- 1/2 teaspoon red pepper flakes
- 1 teaspoon salt

Instructions:
1. Preheat your grill to medium-high heat.
2. In a small bowl, combine the minced garlic, olive oil, red wine vinegar, parsley, oregano, lemon juice, red pepper flakes, and salt and stir to combine.
3. Place the steaks on the grill and cook for about 6 minutes per side, or until desired doneness.
4. When the steaks are done cooking, remove them to a plate and let them rest for a few minutes.
5. Serve the steaks with the chimichurri sauce.

Nutrition information
Serving Size: 1 steak with sauce
Calories: 350
Fat: 28 g
Carbohydrates: 4 g
Protein: 23 g

2. Smoked Pork Ribs with Barbecue Sauce

This delicious and succulent smoked pork ribs recipe with classic barbecue sauce will quickly become one of your favorite go-to meals!
Serving: 4-6
Preparation Time: 30 minutes
Ready Time: 4 hours

Ingredients:
- 4-5 lbs pork ribs
- 2 tablespoons olive oil
- 1 teaspoon black pepper
- 2 tablespoons of your favorite barbecue sauce
- Salt to taste

Instructions:
1. Preheat oven to 225°F.
2. Rub pork ribs with olive oil and season with black pepper and salt.
3. Place ribs in a baking tray and cover with aluminum foil.
4. Bake in preheated oven for 4 hours.
5. Take out of oven and brush the ribs with your favorite barbecue sauce.
6. Preheat barbeque to medium-high heat.
7. Grill the ribs for 10-15 minutes.
8. Serve hot with your favorite sides.
Nutrition Info: 1 serving (1/6th of the recipe) contains 577 calories, 34g fat, 14g saturated fat, 32g carbs, 18g protein.

3. Grilled Chicken Skewers with Lemon Herb Marinade

Grilled Chicken Skewers with Lemon Herb Marinade is an easy and delicious dish. The lemon herb marinade elevates the flavor of the grilled chicken, giving it a zesty and flavorful touch.
Serving: 4
Preparation Time: 10 minutes
Ready Time: 25 minutes

Ingredients:
- 8-10 chicken pieces
- 1/4 cup olive oil
- 1/4 cup lemon juice
- 2 tablespoons minced fresh rosemary
- 2 tablespoons minced fresh thyme
- 2 tablespoons minced fresh oregano
- 1 teaspoon garlic powder
- 1/2 teaspoon each of sea salt and black pepper

Instructions:
1. Combine all the Ingredients for the marinade in a bowl and mix until combined.
2. Place the chicken pieces in a shallow dish and pour marinade over the chicken. Cover with plastic wrap and refrigerate for 15 minutes.
3. Preheat grill to medium-high heat.
4. Thread the chicken onto skewers then place on the hot grill and cook for about 10 minutes, turning every few minutes.
5. Remove the skewers from the grill, let cool for a few minutes, and enjoy!

Nutrition information:
Serving size: 1 skewer
Calories: 222 kcal
Fat: 16 g
Protein: 16 g
Carbohydrates: 3.5 g
Fiber: 1.5 g

4. Smoked Brisket with Homemade Rub

This smoked brisket with homemade rub is a masterpiece of barbecue flavors. Perfectly spiced with a robust rub and smoked to perfection, this flavor-packed dish will quickly become a family favorite.
Serving: 6-8
Preparation time: 35 minutes
Ready time: 8-10 hours

Ingredients:
- 5lb beef brisket
- 1/4 cup smoked paprika
- 2 tablespoons garlic powder
- 2 tablespoons onion powder
- 1 tablespoon ground cumin
- 2 teaspoons ground coriander
- 2 teaspoons black pepper
- 2 teaspoons sea salt
- 2 tablespoons brown sugar
- 2 tablespoons chili powder
- 2 tablespoons olive oil

Instructions:
1. In a small bowl, stir together the smoked paprika, garlic powder, onion powder, cumin, coriander, pepper, salt, brown sugar and chili powder until combined.
2. Rub the brisket all over with olive oil and the prepared spice rub.
3. Transfer the brisket to a preheated smoker set to 225°F.
4. Smoke the brisket for 8-10 hours, or until an instant-read thermometer reads an internal temp of 195°F.
5. Remove the brisket from the smoker and let it rest for 15 minutes before slicing and serving.

Nutrition information: Per serving (based on 8 servings): 369 calories; 14.4 g fat; 38.9 g carbohydrates; 32.2 g protein; 81 mg cholesterol; 573 mg sodium.

5. Grilled Salmon with Dill Sauce

Grilled Salmon with Dill Sauce is a simple and delicious dish for dinner that is prepared in no time. It features tender salmon grilled to perfection with a creamy dill sauce for extra flavor.
Serving: 4
Preparation Time: 10 minutes
Ready Time: 20 minutes

Ingredients:

- 4 salmon fillets
-1/2 teaspoon garlic powder
-1/4 teaspoon black pepper
-1 teaspoon olive oil
-2 tablespoons butter
-2 cloves garlic, minced
-1/2 teaspoon mustard
-2 tablespoons fresh dill, chopped
-1/4 cup dry white wine
-1/4 cup heavy cream

Instructions:
1. Preheat grill to medium heat.
2. Rub salmon with garlic powder, black pepper, and olive oil.
3. Place salmon on preheated grill and cook for 6-8 minutes per side, or until the center of the salmon reaches 145 degrees.
4. Meanwhile, in a small saucepan, melt the butter over medium heat.
5. Add garlic and cook until fragrant, about 1 minute.
6. Stir in mustard and dill, then add white wine and reduce heat to medium-low.
7. Allow sauce to simmer for 3-4 minutes, or until the liquid reduces by about half.
8. Stir in cream and cook for another minute, or until the sauce thickens.
9. Serve the salmon with the dill sauce.

Nutrition information:
Calories: 432, Fat: 27.6g, Carbohydrates: 2.2g, Protein: 38.4g

6. Smoked Turkey Breast with Cranberry Glaze

This Smoked Turkey Breast with Cranberry Glaze recipe is a delicious and flavorful dish that is sure to impress your family and friends this holiday season.
Serving: 8
Preparation Time: 15 minutes
Ready Time: 2 hours

Ingredients:

- 1 (5-7 pound) bone-in turkey breast
- 1 tablespoon olive oil
- 1 teaspoon smoked paprika
- 1 teaspoon garlic powder
- 1 teaspoon onion powder
- 1 teaspoon garlic salt
- 1 tablespoon fresh thyme
- 1/4 cup brown sugar
- 1/4 cup maple syrup
- 1 cup cranberry sauce

Instructions:
1. Preheat the smoker to 250 degrees F.
2. Rub the turkey breast with olive oil and season with smoked paprika, garlic powder, onion powder, garlic salt, and fresh thyme.
3. Place the turkey breast in the smoker and smoke for 1 1/2 to 2 hours, or until the internal temperature registers 165 degrees F.
4. In a small saucepan, combine the brown sugar, maple syrup, and cranberry sauce. Cook over medium heat until the mixture comes to a boil. Remove from heat and let cool.
5. Brush the cranberry glaze over the turkey breast and continue smoking for an additional 15 minutes, or until the glaze is heated through.
6. Serve immediately.

Nutrition information: Per Serving (8 servings): Calories: 255, Total Fat: 6 g, Saturated Fat: 2 g, Cholesterol: 56 mg, Sodium: 459 mg, Carbohydrates: 22 g, Fiber: 1 g, Sugar: 18 g, Protein: 24 g.

7. Grilled Shrimp Tacos with Avocado Salsa

This Grilled Shrimp Tacos with Avocado Salsa recipe is the perfect combination of spicy, sweet, and tangy flavors, making it a great dish for a summer dinner.
Serving: 6-8
Preparation time: 25 minutes
Ready time: 30 minutes

Ingredients:

- 1 lb large shrimp, peeled and deveined
- 2 tbsp olive oil
- 2 tsp garlic powder
- 1 tsp smoked paprika
- 2 tsp chili powder
- 1/2 tsp cumin
- 2 avocados
- 1/2 cup diced tomatoes
- 1/4 cup diced red onion
- 2 tbsp chopped cilantro
- 2 limes, juiced
- Salt and pepper, to taste

Instructions:
1. Preheat an outdoor grill to medium-high heat.
2. In a bowl, combine shrimp, olive oil, garlic powder, smoked paprika, chili powder, and cumin. Toss until completely coated.
3. Grill shrimp for 2-3 minutes per side, until just opaque in the center.
4. In a separate bowl, combine avocados, diced tomatoes, red onion, cilantro, lime juice, salt, and pepper. Mix until incorporated.
5. Serve shrimp tacos with avocado salsa on top.

Nutrition information:
Serving size 1/2 cup
Calories: 216
Fat: 14 g
Carbohydrates: 9 g
Protein: 13 g

8. Smoked Pulled Pork Sandwiches with Coleslaw

This classic sandwich beautifully combines sweet, savory, spicy, and tangy flavors in a hearty, pulled pork sandwich. It's the perfect meal for your next backyard gathering or a quick and easy weeknight dinner.
Serving: 4
Preparation Time: 8 hours
Ready Time: 8 hours

Ingredients:
- 2 lb pork shoulder roast
- 2 tablespoons olive oil
- 1 teaspoon garlic powder
- 1 teaspoon onion powder
- 1 teaspoon paprika
- 1 teaspoon salt
- 2 tablespoon light brown sugar
- 1 teaspoon liquid smoke
- 4 hamburger buns
- Coleslaw (shredded cabbage, carrots, mayonnaise, apple cider vinegar, sugar, and salt)

Instructions:
1. In a small bowl, combine garlic powder, onion powder, paprika, salt, and brown sugar. Rub the mixture all over the pork shoulder.
2. Heat the olive oil in a large pot or Dutch oven over medium-high heat. Add the pork shoulder and cook until golden brown on all sides, about 5-7 minutes.
3. Add the liquid smoke and enough water to cover the pork. Reduce heat to medium-low and simmer for 6-8 hours, or until the pork is tender and shreds easily with a fork.
4. Shred the pork with a fork and serve on hamburger buns topped with coleslaw.

Nutrition information: Per serving: 302 calories, 12.8 g fat, 2.7 g saturated fat, 42 g carbohydrate, 20.7 g protein, 4.5 g fiber.

9. Grilled Lamb Chops with Mint Pesto

This hearty dish features juicy lamb chops grilled to perfection and topped with a delightful mint pesto.
Serving: 4
Preparation Time: 15 minutes
Ready Time: 25 minutes

Ingredients:
- 2 tablespoons olive oil

- 2 cloves garlic, minced
- 6 lamb loin chops
- 2 tablespoons freshly minced mint
- 2 tablespoons freshly grated Parmesan cheese
- Salt and freshly ground black pepper, to taste

Instructions:
1. Heat olive oil in a large skillet over medium heat. Add garlic and cook, stirring occasionally, until fragrant, about 2 minutes.
2. Add lamb chops and season with salt and pepper, to taste. Cook until golden brown and slightly pink inside, about 4-5 minutes per side.
3. Meanwhile, in a small bowl, whisk together mint, Parmesan and remaining olive oil.
4. Serve lamb chops warm with mint pesto.

Nutrition information: 290 calories; 15g fat; 7g carbohydrates; 27g protein per serving.

10. Smoked Sausages with Mustard Sauce

Smoked Sausages with Mustard Sauce is a delicious and nutritious meal, perfect for any time of the day. The savory sausages are smoked and served with a tangy mustard sauce.
Serving: 4
Preparation time: 20 minutes
Ready time: 45 minutes

Ingredients:
- 8 beef or pork smoked sausages
- 2 tablespoons mayonnaise
- 2 tablespoons yellow mustard
- 1 tablespoon Dijon mustard
- 1 tablespoon honey
- 2 tablespoons honey
- 2 tablespoons white wine vinegar
- Salt and pepper to taste

Instructions:

1. Preheat oven to 350°F (175°C).
2. Place sausages on a baking sheet and bake for 30 minutes until cooked through.
3. In a medium bowl, whisk together mayonnaise, yellow mustard, Dijon mustard, honey, white wine vinegar, and salt and pepper.
4. Once the sausages are cooked, brush with the mustard sauce.
5. Return to oven and bake for an additional 15 minutes.
6. Serve with additional mustard sauce on the side.

Nutrition information: Calories: 487, Fat: 32g, Saturated fat: 8g, Cholesterol: 108mg, Sodium: 2090mg, Carbohydrates: 15g, Sugar: 9g, Protein: 30g, Fiber: 0g

11. Grilled Vegetables with Balsamic Glaze

Grilled Vegetables with Balsamic Glaze is a simple and delicious vegetarian dish with a hint of smoky flavor from the grill. It's a great side dish for any dinner.
Serving: 6
Preparation time: 10 minutes
Ready time: 15 minutes

Ingredients:
- 2 zucchinis, cut into rounds
- 2 bell peppers (red & yellow), cut into strips
- 1 head of garlic, sliced
- 2 tablespoons olive oil
- 1 tablespoon balsamic vinegar
- Salt and pepper to taste

Instructions:
1. Preheat the grill to medium-high heat.
2. Place the vegetables on a large baking tray and drizzle with olive oil. Sprinkle with salt and pepper.
3. Grill the vegetables for about 8 minutes, turning several times, until they are tender.
4. Drizzle the balsamic vinegar on the vegetables and grill for 1-2 minutes longer.

5. Serve the vegetables hot off the grill with a sprinkle of salt and pepper.

Nutrition information:
Serving of Grilled Vegetables (200g):
Calories: 128kcal, Fat: 6.5g, Carbohydrates: 14.2g, Protein: 2.7g, Fiber: 4.3g, Sugar: 8.8g.

12. Smoked Chicken Wings with Spicy Buffalo Sauce

Smoked Chicken Wings with Spicy Buffalo Sauce is a flavorful classic appetizer. The smoked chicken wings are tossed with spicy buffalo sauce and perfect for your next game day gathering.
Serving: 6-8
Preparation Time: 15 minutes
Ready Time: 2 hours

Ingredients:
- 2 pounds chicken wings
- 2 tablespoons smoked paprika
- 1 tablespoon chili powder
- 2 teaspoons garlic powder
- 2 teaspoons onion powder
- 2 teaspoons dried oregano
- 2 teaspoons kosher salt
- 1/2 teaspoon ground black pepper
- 1/3 cup butter
- 1/3 cup hot sauce
- 2 tablespoons apple cider vinegar
- 1 teaspoon Worcestershire sauce
- 2 tablespoons honey

Instructions:
1. Preheat your oven or smoker to 375 degrees F.
2. Mix the smoked paprika, chili powder, garlic powder, onion powder, dried oregano, kosher salt, and pepper in a bowl.
3. Rub the wings with the spice mix and place them on a baking sheet lined with parchment paper.

4. Bake the wings in the preheated oven or smoker for about 1 hour and 30 minutes, or until the wings are cooked through, flipping the wings halfway through.
5. Meanwhile, melt the butter in a medium saucepan over medium-low heat.
6. Add the hot sauce, vinegar, Worcestershire sauce, and honey to the melted butter, and stir to combine.
7. Simmer the sauce for about 15 minutes, or until the sauce has reduced slightly and thickened.
8. Remove the wings from the oven or smoker and add them to the saucepan.
9. Toss the wings to coat with the sauce.
10. Serve the wings warm with extra sauce on the side.

Nutrition information:
Serving size: 1/6 of recipe, Calories per serving: 333, Total fat: 15.1g, Saturated fat: 6.9g, Cholesterol: 103mg, Sodium: 886mg, Total carbohydrate: 12.3g, Dietary fiber: 2.3g, Sugars: 9.8g, Protein: 27.8g

13. Grilled Portobello Mushrooms with Balsamic Reduction

Juicy and tender, grilled portobello mushrooms are drizzled with a sweet and tangy balsamic reduction for a quick and flavor-packed side dish.
Serving - 4 servings
Preparation Time - 15 minutes
Ready Time - 30 minutes

Ingredients:
- 4 large Portobello mushrooms
- 1/4 cup extra-virgin olive oil
- 1/2 teaspoon garlic salt
- 2 tablespoons balsamic vinegar
- 1 tablespoon Dijon mustard
- Freshly ground black pepper

Instructions:
1. Preheat a grill or grill pan to medium-high heat.

2. Clean the mushrooms and pat dry with paper towels.
3. In a shallow bowl, mix together the olive oil, garlic salt, balsamic vinegar, and Dijon mustard. Add the mushrooms and turn to coat.
4. Grill the mushrooms for about 10 minutes, turning once, until they begin to soften and release their juices.
5. Transfer the mushrooms to a plate. Drizzle the balsamic reduction over the mushrooms and season with freshly ground black pepper.

Nutrition information -
Calories: 167
Fat: 14g
Carbohydrates: 6g
Fiber: 2g
Protein: 3g

14. Smoked Beef Tenderloin with Horseradish Cream

Succulent and tender beef tenderloin meets zesty horseradish cream in this deliciously simple, yet extraordinary, smoked beef tenderloin entree. Perfect for a special dinner, this recipe offers a flavorful and satisfying meal.
Serving: Serves 8
Preparation Time: 15 minutes
Ready Time: 3 1/2 hours

Ingredients:
- 2 teaspoons smoked sea salt
- 2 teaspoons coarsely ground black pepper
- 2 tablespoons olive oil
- 2-3 lb beef tenderloin
- 1/2 cup prepared horseradish
- 1/2 cup sour cream
- 2 tablespoons freshly squeezed lemon juice
- 2 tablespoons chopped fresh chives

Instructions:
1. Preheat your smoker to 300°F.

2. Combine the smoked salt and black pepper in a small bowl and mix together.
3. Brush the olive oil all over the beef tenderloin.
4. Sprinkle the salt and pepper mixture over the beef tenderloin.
5. Place the beef tenderloin on the smoker grate and cook for 2 1/2 hours or until the internal temperature of the beef has reached 140°F.
6. Remove the beef tenderloin from the smoker.
7. Let rest for 10 minutes.
8. In a medium bowl, mix together the horseradish, sour cream, lemon juice, and chives.
9. Slice the beef tenderloin and serve with the horseradish cream.

Nutrition information (per 4oz):
- Calories: 220
- Fat: 10g
- Cholesterol: 75mg
- Sodium: 320mg
- Protein: 25g
- Carbohydrates: 1g

15. Grilled Mahi Mahi with Mango Salsa

Grilled Mahi Mahi with Mango Salsa is a delicious and nutritious dish for dinner. This combination of flavors is sure to please with the sweetness of the mango and the light flavor of the fish.
Serving: 8
Preparation Time: 20 minutes
Ready Time: 30 minutes

Ingredients:
- 4 (6-ounce) Mahi Mahi fillets
- 2 tablespoons olive oil
- 2 tablespoons freshly squeezed lime juice
- Salt and freshly ground black pepper
- 2 ripe mangoes, peeled and chopped
- 1/2 red pepper, diced
- 1 small red onion, diced
- 1/4 cup fresh cilantro, finely chopped

- 1 jalapeño, seeded and finely diced
- 2 tablespoons freshly squeezed lime juice
- 1/4 teaspoon salt

Instructions:
1. Preheat the grill to medium-high heat.
2. In a bowl, combine the olive oil, lime juice, salt, and pepper. Rub the mixture onto the Mahi Mahi fillets.
3. Grill the fish for 3 - 4 minutes per side, until cooked through.
4. In a separate bowl, combine the mangoes, red pepper, red onion, cilantro, jalapeño, lime juice, and salt. Stir to combine.
5. Serve the grilled mahi mahi with the mango salsa on top.

Nutrition information: Per serving: 241 calories, 14.7 g fat, 5.7 g saturated fat, 4.3 g carbohydrates, 0.6 g sugar, 21.7 g protein, 1.7 g fiber

16. Smoked Baby Back Ribs with Honey Glaze

Just the thought of juicy, smoky, succulent smoked baby back ribs smothered in a honey glaze sounds great, right? But the preparation can take some time. This recipe will show you how to make delicious smoked baby back ribs with a honey glaze that will make your mouth water.
Serving: Serves 4
Preparation time: 18 hours
Ready time: 6 hours

Ingredients:
- 1 rack of baby back ribs
- 2 tablespoons of garlic powder
- 2 tablespoons of onion powder
- 1 tablespoon of paprika
- 1 tablespoon of chili powder
- 2 tablespoons of brown sugar
- 2 tablespoons of salt
- 4 tablespoons of olive oil
- 2 cups of honey

Instructions:
1. Preheat the smoker to 225 degrees Fahrenheit.
2. In a small bowl, mix garlic powder, onion powder, paprika, chili powder, brown sugar and salt together.
3. Rub the ribs with olive oil and the spice mixture.
4. Place the ribs in the smoker and cook for 4-6 hours.
5. Once the ribs are cooked, carefully transfer them to a baking sheet.
6. Preheat the oven to 400 degrees Fahrenheit.
7. Brush the ribs with honey and bake for 15-20 minutes.
8. Move the ribs to a platter or cutting board.
9. Slice and serve.

Nutrition information: per serving – 536 calories, 29.8g fat, 37.4g protein, 31.5g carbohydrates, 2.2g fiber.

17. Grilled Teriyaki Chicken Skewers

Grilled Teriyaki Chicken Skewers are the perfect summer recipe. This easy and delicious meal is marinated in a homemade teriyaki sauce and then grilled to perfection.
Serving: 4
Preparation Time: 30 minutes
Ready Time: 30 minutes

Ingredients:
- 4 boneless skinless chicken breasts, cut into 1-inch cubes
-1 cup of teriyaki sauce
-4 bamboo skewers, soaked in water for 30 minutes

Instructions:
1. Combine teriyaki sauce and chicken cubes in a large bowl. Mix well to ensure all pieces of chicken are fully coated in the marinade.
2. Thread chicken cubes onto soaked skewers, and place onto a preheated grill over medium-high heat.
3. Grill chicken skewers for approximately 10 minutes, flipping once, until lightly charred and chicken centres are cooked through.
4. Serve warm over steamed rice or with a fresh green salad.

Nutrition information: per serving (4 skewers): 291 calories, 8.2g fat, 8.3g carbohydrates, 39.7g protein.

18. Smoked Pork Belly Burnt Ends

Smoked Pork Belly Burnt Ends is a delicious and savory dish with a smoky flavor that makes it a wonderful addition to your meal. This recipe is sure to be a hit with your family and friends!
Serving: 8
Preparation time: 10 minutes
Ready time: 3-4 hours

Ingredients:
- 4-5 pounds pork belly
- 1 cup of brown sugar
- 1/2 cup BBQ sauce
- 1/2 cup honey
- Salt and pepper

Instructions:
1. Preheat the smoker to 225 degrees.
2. Cut the pork belly into 2-inch cubes.
3. Generously season the cubes with salt and pepper.
4. Place the cubes in the smoker and cook for 2-3 hours, until the internal temperature reaches 165 degrees
5. In a bowl add the brown sugar, BBQ sauce, and honey. Mix together until smooth.
6. Brush the pork cubes with the glaze.
7. Return the pork cubes to the smoker and cook for 1 more hour.
8. Once done, remove the pork cubes and let them cool before serving.

Nutrition information: 200 Calories, 10g Fat, 10g Carbs, 12g Protein

19. Grilled Vegetable Kabobs with Herb Marinade

Enjoy the smoky flavor of the grill with this delicious and healthy recipe for Grilled Vegetable Kabobs with Herb Marinade. Serve with a side of rice and you have a fantastic meal!

Serving: 6 servings
Preparation Time: 10 minutes
Ready Time: 40 minutes

Ingredients:
- 1/3 cup olive oil
- 3 tablespoons fresh lemon juice
- 2 tablespoons Dijon mustard
- 2 garlic cloves, minced
- 1 teaspoon dried oregano
- 2 teaspoons dried dill
- 2 teaspoons dried rosemary
- 1/2 teaspoon ground black pepper
- 1/2 teaspoon salt
- 1 red onion, cut into wedges
- 1 green bell pepper, cut into 1-inch pieces
- 1 yellow bell pepper, cut into 1-inch pieces
- 2 cups baby Portobello mushrooms
- 2 cups cherry tomatoes
- 12 large metal or wooden skewers

Instructions:
1. In a small bowl, whisk together olive oil, lemon juice, Dijon mustard, garlic, oregano, dill, rosemary, black pepper and salt.
2. Place the onion, bell pepper, mushrooms and tomatoes into a large bowl. Pour the marinade over the vegetables and toss to coat. Cover and let marinate in the refrigerator for 30 minutes to one hour.
3. Preheat an outdoor grill for high heat.
4. Thread the marinated vegetables onto the skewers, alternating vegetables until all are used.
5. Lightly oil the grate. Grill the vegetables for 8-10 minutes, turning once, until vegetables are tender but still slightly firm.

Nutrition information: Calorie 247, Protein 4g, Carbs 19g, Fat 17g, Sodium 421mg, Fiber 4g

20. Smoked Salmon with Lemon Dill Butter

Smoked Salmon with Lemon Dill Butter is a delicious and easy to make meal featuring smoked salmon topped with butter flavored with lemon, dill, and other herbs for a zesty flavor.
Serving: 4
Preparation Time: 10 minutes
Ready Time: 10 minutes

Ingredients:
- 4 smoked salmon fillets
- 2 tablespoons of lemon juice
- 2 tablespoons of melted butter
- 2 tablespoons of fresh dill, chopped
- 1 tablespoon of garlic, minced
- 1 teaspoon of pepper
- Salt to taste

Instructions:
1. Preheat oven to 375 degrees.
2. Place salmon fillets on a greased baking sheet.
3. In a small bowl, mix together lemon juice, melted butter, dill, garlic, pepper, and salt.
4. Spread the butter mixture over the salmon fillets.
5. Bake for 8-10 minutes or until salmon is cooked through.

Nutrition information:
Calories: 180,
Fat: 10g,
Carbohydrates: 1g,
Protein: 21g

21. Grilled Ribeye Steak with Herb Butter

Grilled Ribeye Steak with Herb Butter is a classic steakhouse recipe that is sure to impress your dinner guests. The tender steak, seasoned with garlic, pepper, and thyme, is cooked to perfection and served topped with homemade herb-infused butter that adds a rich and savory element.

Serving: 2
Preparation Time: 10 minutes
Ready Time: 15 minutes

Ingredients:
- 2 boneless ribeye steaks
- 2 cloves garlic, minced
- 1 teaspoon freshly ground black pepper
- 2 tablespoons fresh thyme leaves, chopped
- 2 tablespoons butter, softened
- 2 tablespoons fresh parsley, finely chopped
- 1 tablespoon fresh chives, minced
- 1 teaspoon extra virgin olive oil

Instructions:
- Heat a grill or grill pan to medium-high heat.
- Rub one side of each steak with garlic, black pepper, and thyme.
- Place the steaks on the grill, seasoned side down, and cook for 4 to 6 minutes, or until the steak is golden brown on the bottom.
- Flip the steaks and cook for an additional 3 to 5 minutes, or until the steak is cooked to your desired doneness.
- Remove the steaks from the grill and let rest for 5 minutes.
- Meanwhile, stir together the butter, parsley, chives, and olive oil in a small bowl until well blended.
- Serve the steaks topped with the herb butter.

Nutrition information:
Calories: 260; Fat: 11; Protein: 37; Carbs: 1; Sodium: 344

22. Smoked Chicken Thighs with BBQ Dry Rub

Delicious, smoky-spicy and succulent chicken thighs made with a custom dry rub and slow cooked in a smoker complete this backyard bbq favorite.
Serving: 4
Preparation time: 15 minutes
Ready time: 1 hour 10 minutes

Ingredients:
- 4 boneless chicken thighs
- 1 teaspoon garlic powder
- 1 teaspoon smoked paprika
- ½ teaspoon each of Worcestershire sauce, onion powder, ground black pepper and salt
- 2 tablespoons olive oil
- 2 tablespoons brown sugar

Instructions:
1. In a bowl, mix together garlic powder, smoked paprika, Worcestershire sauce, onion powder, ground black pepper and salt.
2. Rub olive oil on the chicken thighs and rub the dry rub mix onto the chicken thighs.
3. Place chicken on a dish and sprinkle brown sugar on top.
4. Preheat a smoker to 275°F and place the chicken in the smoker.
5. Allow the chicken to smoke for 45 minutes.
6. Increase the heat of the smoker to 350°F and allow the chicken to smoke for 20 minutes more until cooked through.
7. Slice and serve with favorite BBQ sides.

Nutrition information: (Per serving): Calories: 235; Total Fat: 14g; Saturated Fat: 3g; Sodium: 545mg; Carbohydrates: 4g; Fiber: 0.5g; Sugar: 2g; Protein: 24g.

23. Grilled Swordfish with Lemon Caper Sauce

Grilled Swordfish with Lemon Caper Sauce is a perfect dish for a summer evening on the grill. The swordfish is simply seasoned and seared to perfection and the buttery lemon caper sauce complements it perfectly.
Serving: 4
Preparation time: 10 minutes
Ready time: 30 minutes

Ingredients:
- 4 swordfish steaks, 1/2 inch thick
- 2 tablespoons olive oil

- 2 teaspoons coarse salt
- 1 teaspoon freshly ground black pepper
- 2 tablespoons butter
- 2 tablespoons capers, drained
- 2 tablespoons freshly squeezed lemon juice
- 1 tablespoon chopped fresh parsley

Instructions:
1. Preheat grill to medium-high heat.
2. Rinse swordfish steaks under cold water and pat dry. Brush with olive oil, then sprinkle salt and black pepper over top.
3. Place swordfish steaks on preheated grill and cook for 4-5 minutes per side, or until fish reaches desired doneness.
4. Meanwhile, melt butter in a small saucepan over low heat. Add capers and lemon juice and stir until combined.
5. Remove cookedswordfish from grill and spoon lemon caper sauce over top. Sprinkle parsley on top and serve.

Nutrition information:
Serving size: 4
Calories: 214 kcal
Fat: 11 g
Carbohydrates: 2 g
Protein: 25 g

24. Smoked Bratwurst with Beer Braised Onions

Smoked Bratwurst with Beer Braised Onions is a classic German dish that combines smoky bratwurst sausages and tender, flavorful onions cooked in a savory beer broth. It's perfect for an outdoor dinner party, large gathering, or a relaxed family meal.
Serving: 4
Preparation time: 10 minutes
Ready time: 45 minutes

Ingredients:
- 4 smoked bratwurst
- 2 tablespoons olive oil

- 2 onions, sliced
- 1 beer
- Salt and pepper

Instructions:
1. Heat olive oil in a large skillet over medium heat.
2. Add the onions and sauté for 5 minutes.
3. Pour in the beer and bring to a boil.
4. Add the bratwurst and reduce the heat to medium-low. Simmer, covered, for 30 minutes.
5. Season with salt and pepper, to taste.
6. Serve hot.

Nutrition information: Per serving: 252 calories, 13g fat, 9g carbohydrates, 18g protein

25. Grilled Asparagus with Parmesan Cheese

Grilled Asparagus with Parmesan Cheese is a delicious side dish. The asparagus is lightly grilled to perfection and topped with melted Parmesan cheese for an extra touch of flavor.
Serving - This recipe serves 2 people.
Preparation Time - 10 minutes
Ready Time - 15 minutes

Ingredients:
- 6 tablespoons olive oil
- 1 teaspoon garlic, minced
- 2 bunches asparagus, trimmed
- Salt & pepper to taste
- 1/3 cup freshly grated Parmesan cheese, plus more for garnish

Instructions:
1. Preheat your oven to 375°F (190°C).
2. Heat the olive oil in a large skillet or baking dish over medium-high heat.
3. Add the garlic and cook for about 1 minute, until fragrant.

4. Add the asparagus to the pan and season with salt and pepper to taste.

5. Saute for 3–4 minutes, until the asparagus is lightly charred and tender.

6. Transfer the asparagus to a baking dish and top with the Parmesan cheese.

7. Bake in the preheated oven for 10 minutes, or until the Parmesan cheese is melted and golden.

8. Transfer the asparagus to a serving dish and garnish with more freshly grated Parmesan cheese. Serve.

Nutrition information -
- Calories - 230 kcal per Serving:
- Fat - 16.4g
- Carbs - 8.3 g
- Protein - 9.4g

26. Smoked Beef Ribs with Espresso BBQ Sauce

Enjoy the rich and smoky flavor of smoked beef ribs combined with a thick and slightly sweet espresso BBQ sauce. This delicious dish is perfect for grilling during the summer months and will draw in compliments from everyone!
Serving: 4
Preparation time: 10 minutes
Ready time: 3 hours

Ingredients:
- 2 lbs. beef ribs
- 2 cups espresso BBQ sauce
- 2 teaspoons smoked paprika
- 2 teaspoons garlic powder
- Salt and pepper, to taste

Instructions:
1. Preheat your grill to medium heat.
2. In a shallow bowl, combine espresso BBQ sauce, smoked paprika, and garlic powder.

3. Season ribs with salt and pepper to taste and coat with the espresso BBQ sauce mixture.
4. Place ribs on the grill and cook for 2 to 3 hours, flipping and basting with sauce every 30 minutes until cooked through.
5. Remove ribs from the grill when done and serve with your favorite side dishes.

Nutrition information: (Per Serving)
Calories: 825
Carbohydrates: 8g
Protein: 48g
Fat: 64g
Saturated Fat: 24g
Cholesterol: 195mg
Sodium: 881mg
Potassium: 605mg
Fiber: 0g
Sugar: 4g
Vitamin A: 803IU
Vitamin C: 3mg
Calcium: 50mg
Iron: 3mg

27. Grilled Shrimp Scampi with Garlic Butter

Grilled Shrimp Scampi with Garlic Butter is an easy and delicious seafood dish with a pleasant combination of herbs and spices, served with a creamy garlic butter sauce.
Serving: 4
Preparation Time: 5 minutes
Ready Time: 25 minutes

Ingredients:
- 1 lb uncooked shrimp (peeled and de-veined)
- 2 tablespoons olive oil
- 2 tablespoons lemon juice
- 2 cloves minced garlic
- 2 tablespoons fresh parsley, chopped

- 1 teaspoon oregano
- 1/2 teaspoon red pepper flakes
- Salt and pepper to taste
- 1/4 cup butter
- 1/4 cup freshly grated Parmesan cheese

Instructions:
1. Preheat your grill to a medium-hot heat.
2. In a medium-sized bowl, combine olive oil, lemon juice, garlic, parsley, oregano, red pepper flakes, salt, and pepper. Mix together to combine.
3. Add the shrimp to the bowl and stir to make sure each piece is well-coated with the marinade.
4. Place the shrimp on the preheated grill and cook 4-5 minutes per side or until they are golden brown and cooked through.
5. In a separate small saucepan, melt the butter over medium heat.
6. Once the butter is melted, add the Parmesan cheese and stir until combined.
7. Once everything is combined, remove from heat and serve over the cooked shrimp.

Nutrition information:
Calories: 287 | Total Fat: 18g | Saturated Fat: 9g | Cholesterol: 155mg | Sodium: 552mg | Total Carbohydrates: 3g | Dietary Fiber: 1g | Protein: 26g

28. Smoked Duck Breast with Orange Glaze

This Smoked Duck Breast with Orange Glaze is a combination of savory and sweet that your entire family will love! The combination of smoky flavor and sweet orange glaze is simply delicious!
Serving: 4
Preparation Time: 10 minutes
Ready Time: 45 minutes

Ingredients:
- 4 duck breasts
- 2 tablespoons olive oil
- 2 tablespoons garlic, minced

- 2 tablespoons smoked paprika
- 1/4 cup orange juice
- 2 tablespoons honey
- 2 tablespoons balsamic vinegar
- Salt and pepper to taste

Instructions:
1. Preheat your smoker to 250 degrees Fahrenheit.
2. Rub the duck breasts with the olive oil, garlic, and smoked paprika.
3. Place the duck breasts on the smoker, cover, and smoke for 45 minutes.
4. While the duck is cooking, combine the orange juice, honey, and balsamic vinegar in a small saucepan and bring to a simmer. Simmer until the sauce thickens.
5. Once the duck is done cooking, brush with the orange glaze.
6. Serve the duck breasts with your favorite sides.

Nutrition information:
Calories: 346 kcal
Total Fat: 18.6 g
Saturated Fat: 4.3 g
Cholesterol: 101 mg
Sodium: 64 mg
Carbohydrates: 12.2 g
Fiber: 0.7 g
Sugar: 9.3 g
Protein: 32.5 g

29. Grilled Zucchini with Feta and Mint

Try out something new and delicious with this Grilled Zucchini with Feta and Mint recipe! A perfect summer side dish that is easy to make.
Serving: 4
Preparation Time: 15 minutes
Ready Time: 25 minutes

Ingredients:
• 4 small zucchini, cut into long slices

- 2 tablespoons olive oil
- 1 tablespoon balsamic vinegar
- 2 tablespoons crumbled feta
- 2 tablespoons chopped fresh mint
- Salt and freshly ground black pepper
- 1 tablespoon toasted pine nuts

Instructions:
1. Preheat a grill or grill pan to medium-high heat.
2. In a bowl, mix together the olive oil and balsamic vinegar.
3. Place the zucchini slices on a plate or baking sheet and brush with the olive oil/balsamic vinegar mixture.
4. Grill the zucchini on both sides until lightly charred, about 2-3 minutes per side.
5. Transfer to a serving plate and top with feta, mint, salt and pepper, and toasted pine nuts.
6. Serve warm.

Nutrition information:
Calories: 106, Fat: 7.5g, Cholesterol: 6mg, Sodium: 155mg, Carbohydrates: 6.2g, Fiber: 1.9g, Protein: 4.1g

30. Smoked St Louis Style Ribs with Sweet and Spicy Rub

Smoked St. Louis Style Ribs with Sweet and Spicy Rub is a finger-licking dish that makes a delicious main course. This mouthwatering recipe combines sweet and spicy flavors for a delicious treat.
Serving: 8
Preparation Time: 10 minutes
Ready Time: 5 hours

Ingredients:
-4 lb St. Louis Style Ribs
-3 tablespoons dark brown sugar
-2 tablespoons garlic powder
-1 teaspoon ground ginger
-1 teaspoon smoked paprika

-1/4 teaspoon cayenne pepper
-1 teaspoon onion powder
-2 tablespoons salt
-1 teaspoon black pepper

Instructions:
1. Mix the dark brown sugar, garlic powder, ground ginger, smoked paprika, cayenne pepper, onion powder, salt and pepper in a bowl.
2. Take the ribs out and dry them off, then liberally apply the rub.
3. Preheat your smoker to 250°F and add your favorite hardwood chips for added flavor.
4. Place the ribs on the smoker grate and close the lid.
5. Keep an eye on the internal temperature of the ribs, and when they reach 205°F internal temperature, they're done.
6. Serve and enjoy!

Nutrition information:
Calories: 267, Carbohydrates: 15g, Protein: 22g, Fat: 12g, Saturated Fat: 4g, Cholesterol: 66mg, Sodium: 1454mg, Potassium: 271mg, Sugar: 9g, Vitamin A: 327IU, Calcium: 42mg, Iron: 1mg.

31. Grilled Chicken Caesar Salad

A wholesome mix of lettuce, grilled chicken, croutons and parmesan cheese topped with Caesar dressing, this Grilled Chicken Caesar Salad is packed with flavor and nutrition.
Serving: 4-6
Preparation Time: 15 minutes
Ready Time: 15 minutes

Ingredients:
- 2 heads Romaine lettuce, washed and chopped
- 2 medium sized chicken breasts, grilled and thinly sliced
- 2 tablespoons olive oil
- 1/4 cup croutons
- 2 tablespoons parmesan cheese, freshly grated
- 1/4 cup Caesar salad dressing

Instructions:
1. Preheat the oven to 350°F and prepare the grilled chicken.
2. Place the chopped Romaine lettuce in a large salad bowl.
3. Drizzle olive oil over the Romaine lettuce and toss to coat.
4. Add the croutons and parmesan cheese to the lettuce.
5. Top with the grilled chicken slices.
6. Drizzle the Caesar salad dressing over the salad and toss to combine.

Nutrition information:
Serving Size: 1/4 recipe
Calories: 164 kcal
Fat: 9.7 g
Carbohydrates: 5.8 g
Fiber: 1.3 g
Protein: 13.3 g

32. Smoked Pork Shoulder with Carolina BBQ Sauce

Smoked Pork Shoulder with Carolina BBQ Sauce is a delicious and easy to make meal perfect for any summer cookout. The combination of flavorful pork, tangy barbecue sauce and a hint of smokiness from the slow-cooking method makes this dish irresistibly mouthwatering.
Serving: 4-6
Preparation Time: 30 minutes
Ready Time: 4-5 hours

Ingredients:
- 4-5 lb. pork shoulder
- 2 cups Carolina BBQ sauce
- 2 tablespoons garlic powder
- 2 tablespoons onion powder
- 2 tablespoons smoked paprika
- 2 tablespoons pepper
- 2 tablespoons salt

Instructions:
1. Preheat the smoker to 225°F.

2. Rub the pork shoulder with garlic powder, onion powder, smoked paprika, pepper, and salt.
3. Place the pork shoulder on the smoker and slow-cook for 4-5 hours until the internal temperature reads 160°F.
4. Remove the pork shoulder from the smoker and let it rest for 10-15 minutes.
5. Shred the pork and add the Carolina BBQ sauce. Stir it until the pork is fully coated.
6. Serve the pork with any sides of your choice.

Nutrition information: Serving size 4-6; Calories: 589 kcal; Protein: 47.4 g; Carbohydrates: 17.3 g; Fat: 34.3 g; Cholesterol: 134.2 mg; Sodium: 1418.2 mg; Fiber: 2.3 g

33. Grilled Pineapple with Brown Sugar Glaze

Grill Pineapple with Brown Sugar Glaze is a delicious warm summer dessert that is sweet, juicy, and has a slight smoky taste from the grill. Not only is it easy to make, but it's also a healthy and refreshing treat that will always be a hit!
Serving: 4
Preparation Time: 10 minutes
Ready Time: 25 minutes

Ingredients:
- 1 Pineapple, sliced into 1 inch thick pieces
- 2 tbsp Brown Sugar
- 2 tbsp Butter, melted
- 2 tsp Ground Cinnamon
- 1/4 tsp Ground Nutmeg

Instructions:
1. Preheat the grill to medium-high heat.
2. In a medium bowl, combine the brown sugar, melted butter, cinnamon, and nutmeg until blended.
3. Place the pineapple slices on the grill and brush the brown sugar mixture over each slice.

4. Grill for 10-12 minutes or until the pineapple are slightly charred and tender, flipping halfway.
5. Serve warm.

Nutrition information:
Calories: 98 kcal; Carbohydrates: 20 g; Protein: 0.5 g; Fat: 3.5 g; Saturated Fat: 2 g; Trans Fat: 0 g; Cholesterol: 8 mg; Sodium: 26 mg; Fiber: 2 g; Sugar: 17 g.

34. Smoked Lamb Racks with Rosemary Garlic Marinade

This delicious and succulent dish pairs perfectly juicy racks of lamb with a rosemary garlic marinade, smoked to perfection.
Serving: 4
Preparation Time: 15 minutes
Ready Time: 1 hour

Ingredients:
- 4 racks of lamb
- 2 tablespoons olive oil
- 2 cloves of garlic, minced
- 2 tablespoons minced fresh rosemary
- 1 teaspoon black pepper
- 1 teaspoon sea salt

Instructions:
1. Preheat your smoker to 225°F.
2. In a small bowl, mix together olive oil, garlic, rosemary, black pepper, and sea salt.
3. Place the lamb racks in a shallow dish and pour the marinade over them. Let the racks marinate for 30 minutes.
4. Place the racks of lamb on the smoker and reduce the temperature to 180°F.
5. Smoke the lamb racks for about 40 minutes until they reach an internal temperature of 145°F.
6. Let the lamb racks rest for 5 minutes before serving.

Nutrition information: Per 4 Rack Serving: 543 calories; 41 g fat; 9 g carbohydrates; 33 g protein; 1 g fiber; 295 mg sodium.

35. Grilled Halloumi Skewers with Lemon Herb Dressing

Grilled Halloumi Skewers with Lemon Herb Dressing is an easy and delicious recipe made with lemon, herbs and grilled halloumi cheese. It is perfect to serve as a light lunch or snack.
Serving: 4
Preparation Time: 10 minutes
Ready Time: 15 minutes

Ingredients:
 - 250g halloumi cheese, cut into 2.5cm cubes
 - 1 tablespoon olive oil
 - 1 garlic clove, minced
 - 2 tablespoons chopped fresh herbs (e.g. thyme, oregano, rosemary, basil)
 - Zest and juice of 1 lemon
 - Salt and pepper to taste

Instructions:
1. Preheat the grill to medium-high heat.
2. Place the halloumi cubes in a bowl and toss with olive oil, garlic, herbs, zest and juice of the lemon. Season with salt and pepper.
3. Skewer the halloumi cubes and place them on the preheated grill for 5-7 minutes, or until golden brown.
4. Serve with a side of the lemon herb dressing.

Nutrition information:
Per serving: Calories 173, Fat 12g, Carbs 2g, Protein 15g

36. Smoked Corned Beef with Mustard Glaze

Smoked Corned Beef with Mustard Glaze is an easy and delicious dish that can be prepared in no time. It's a perfect choice for any special occasion.
Serving: 6-8
Preparation Time: 25 minutes
Ready Time: 3 hours

Ingredients:
- 4 lb corned beef
- 1/4 cup Dijon mustard
- 1 tsp garlic powder
- 1/2 tsp cayenne pepper
- 1/2 cup brown sugar
- 1/4 cup honey
- 1/4 cup apple cider vinegar

Instructions:
1. Preheat oven to 275 degrees. Place the corned beef in a large roasting pan.
2. In a small bowl, mix together mustard, garlic powder, cayenne pepper, brown sugar, honey, and cider vinegar until well combined.
3. Spread the mustard glaze over the corned beef. Cover the roasting pan with foil.
4. Place in oven and bake for 2 1/2 to 3 hours until the internal temperature of the corned beef reaches 160 degrees.
5. Remove from oven and let cool before cutting.

Nutrition information:
Per Serving (6 oz): 330 calories, 20g total fat, 6g saturated fat, 90mg sodium, 15g carbohydrate, 6g protein

37. Grilled Eggplant with Tahini Sauce

Grilled Eggplant with Tahini Sauce is a delicious vegetarian meal featuring slices of smoky grilled eggplant served with a creamy garlic and lemon tahini sauce.
Serving: Makes 4 servings
Preparation time: 10 minutes

Ready time: 20 minutes

Ingredients:
- 1 large eggplant, 1/4-inch slices
- 2 tablespoons extra-virgin olive oil
- Salt and freshly ground black pepper to taste
- 4 tablespoons tahini
- 2-3 tablespoons freshly squeezed lemon juice
- 2 cloves garlic, minced
- 2 tablespoons warm water
- 1 tablespoon chopped fresh parsley (optional)

Instructions:
1. Preheat the grill to medium-high heat.
2. Brush the eggplant slices with olive oil. Season with salt and pepper.
3. Grill the eggplant slices for 2 to 3 minutes per side, until lightly charred and heated through.
4. Meanwhile, combine the tahini, lemon juice, and garlic in a small bowl and mix until combined.
5. Gradually add the warm water to the tahini mixture and continue to mix until smooth.
6. Place the grilled eggplant slices on a serving plate and top with the tahini sauce. Garnish with fresh parsley (optional).

Nutrition information:
Serving Size: 1 slice of eggplant topped with 2 tablespoons of tahini sauce
Calories: 145.3
Total Fat: 6.0g
Cholesterol: 0mg
Sodium: 6.7mg
Total Carbohydrates: 13.6g
Dietary Fiber: 4.1g
Protein: 6.6g

38. Smoked Sausage and Peppers

Smoked Sausage and Peppers is an easy and flavorful comfort food that will make you eat for hours. Prepared with smoked sausage, bell peppers, and onion, this dish is sure to delight your taste buds.

Serving: 4
Preparation Time: 10 minutes
Ready Time: 35 minutes

Ingredients:
- 2 tablespoons of olive oil
- 2 red, yellow, or green bell peppers, diced
- 1 yellow onion, diced
- 3 cloves of garlic, minced
- 1 pound of smoked sausage, sliced
- 2 tablespoons of Worcestershire sauce
- 1 teaspoon of Italian seasoning
- Salt and black pepper to taste

Instructions:
1. Preheat the oven to 350°F.
2. Heat the olive oil in large oven-safe skillet over medium-high heat.
3. Add the bell peppers and onion to the skillet and cook for 5 minutes until softened.
4. Add the garlic and cook for an additional minute.
5. Add the sausage and cook for 5 minutes.
6. Add the Worcestershire sauce, Italian seasoning, salt, and pepper. Stir to combine.
7. Transfer the skillet to the preheated oven and bake for 20 minutes.

Nutrition information: Per Serving: Calories 408, Total Fat 23g (Saturated 5g, Trans 0g), Cholesterol 73mg, Sodium 1067mg, Total Carbohydrate 22g (Dietary Fiber 4g, Sugars 6g), Protein 25g, Vitamin D 0%, Calcium 6%, Iron 12%, Potassium 537mg.

39. Grilled Tandoori Chicken with Yogurt Marinade

This grilled tandoori chicken with yogurt marinade is a wonderfully flavorful and succulent dish. Perfect for a light lunch or dinner, the yogurt marinade gives the protein a subtly tangy flavor and leaves the meat tender and juicy.

Serving: 4

Preparation Time: 15 minutes

Ready Time: 1 hour 30 minutes

Ingredients:
- 4 chicken breasts
- 1 cup plain yogurt
- 2 tablespoons olive oil
- 1 teaspoon ground cumin
- 1 teaspoon garam masala
- 1 teaspoon ground garlic
- 1 teaspoon ground coriander
- 1 teaspoon ground mint
- Juice of 1 lemon
- Salt and pepper to taste

Instructions:

1. In a large bowl, whisk together the yogurt, olive oil, cumin, garam masala, garlic, coriander, and mint.
2. Place the chicken breasts in the marinade and coat well. Cover and chill for at least 1 hour, up to overnight.
3. Preheat your grill to medium-high heat.
4. Once the grill is hot, remove the chicken from the marinade and season with salt and pepper. Grill chicken for 10-12 minutes, flipping every few minutes, until the chicken is fully cooked.
5. Serve with extra lemon juice, if desired.

Nutrition information: (Per Serving)
Calories: 200, Fat: 10g, Protein: 25g, Carbohydrates: 4g, Fiber: 1g, Sodium: 70mg

40. Smoked Prime Rib with Herb Crust

A classic dish, smoked prime rib with herb crust is a tantalizing addition to any special dinner. The rib is smoked to add flavor and crispness to

the crust and the herbs give it a final flourish. Serve with roasted vegetables and mashed potatoes for a memorable meal.
Serving: 8
Preparation time: 15 minutes
Ready time: 3 1/2 hours

Ingredients:
* 3/4 cup olive oil
* 2 tablespoons chopped fresh rosemary
* 2 tablespoons chopped fresh thyme
* 2 tablespoons chopped fresh sage
* 4 cloves garlic, minced
* 2 teaspoons paprika
* 1 teaspoon onion powder
* 1 teaspoon garlic powder
* 1 teaspoon black pepper
* 3 1/2 pound boneless prime rib

Instructions:
1. Preheat oven to 250°F.
2. In a small bowl, mix together olive oil, rosemary, thyme, sage, garlic, paprika, onion powder, garlic powder, and black pepper.
3. Rub herb mixture over the prime rib.
4. Place prime rib in a roasting pan or on a rack.
5. Place in preheated oven and cook for 3 1/2 hours.
6. Let rest for 10 minutes before slicing.

Nutrition information: Serving size: 1/8 of prime rib. Calories: 200, Total Fat: 12g, Cholesterol: 50mg, Sodium: 480mg, Total Carbohydrate: 2g, Dietary Fiber: 0g, Protein: 21g.

41. Grilled Watermelon Salad with Feta and Mint

Grilled Watermelon Salad with Feta and Mint is an easy and delicious summer salad! It's fresh, zingy, sweet and juicy with a combination of grilled watermelon, feta, and fresh mint.
Serving: 4
Preparation Time: 5 minutes

Ready Time: 15 minutes

Ingredients:
- 4 cups diced watermelon
- 2 tablespoons olive oil
- Salt and pepper to taste
- 4 ounces feta cheese, crumbled
- 2 tablespoons fresh mint leaves, chopped
- 2 tablespoons balsamic vinegar

Instructions:
1. Preheat your grill to medium-high heat.
2. Toss the diced watermelon with the olive oil, salt and pepper.
3. Grill the watermelon for 8-10 minutes, flipping occasionally until lightly charred.
4. To assemble the salad, place the grilled watermelon in a large bowl.
5. Add the crumbled feta, chopped mint, and balsamic vinegar.
6. Gently toss to combine.

Nutrition information: (per serving) 180 calories, 11g fat, 8g carbohydrates, 10g protein

42. Smoked Chicken Drumsticks with Spicy Rub

These delicious smoked chicken drumsticks are seasoned with a simple, yet flavorful, spicy rub that adds the perfect amount of heat and complexity. Serve along with your favorite side dish and you have a delicious meal for your guests!
Serving: 4
Preparation Time: 10 minutes
Ready Time: 2 hours

Ingredients:
- 4 chicken drumsticks
- 1 tablespoon olive oil
- 2 teaspoons paprika
- 1 teaspoon garlic powder
- 1 teaspoon cumin

- 1 teaspoon smoked sea salt
- 1 teaspoon chili powder
- 1/4 teaspoon black pepper

Instructions:
1. Preheat the smoker to 225 degrees F.
2. In a small bowl, mix together the olive oil, paprika, garlic powder, cumin, smoked sea salt, chili powder, and black pepper.
3. Rub the chicken drumsticks with the spice mixture, coating them evenly.
4. Place the chicken drumsticks in the smoker and cook for 1 hour and 45 minutes, or until the internal temperature reaches 165 degrees F.
5. Serve with your favorite side dish.

Nutrition information:
- Calories: 140
- Protein: 9g
- Fat: 9g
- Carbohydrates: 1g
- Fiber: 0g
- Sodium: 430mg

43. Grilled Scallops with Lemon Butter Sauce

Grilled scallops with lemon butter sauce is a simple yet flavorful dish perfect for a seafood dinner. The crisp grilled scallops are enhanced by the creamy lemon butter sauce which adds the perfect hint of sweetness.
Serving: 4
Preparation time: 10 minutes
Ready time: 25 minutes

Ingredients:
-16 large sea scallops, thawed
-4 tablespoon unsalted butter, melted
-2 tablespoon freshly squeezed lemon juice
-2 tablespoons chopped parsley
-Salt and pepper to taste

Instructions:
1. Preheat an outdoor grill to medium-high heat. Grease the grill grates lightly with oil.
2. Place scallops in a large bowl and knead them well with salt and pepper.
3. Transfer scallops onto the preheated grill and cook for 4-5 minutes on each side, or until maculated.
4. In a small bowl, stir together the melted butter, lemon juice and parsley.
5. Place the cooked scallops onto a plate and spoon the lemon butter sauce over scallops.

Nutrition information: Calories: 262 per serving, Fat: 19g, Cholesterol: 64mg, Sodium: 95mg, Carbohydrates: 2g, Protein: 20g.

44. Smoked Pork Tenderloin with Apple Chutney

This flavorful dish of smoked pork tenderloin with apple chutney is sure to please. The tender pork combined with the sweet and tart apple chutney has a beautiful flavor combination.
Serving: Serves 4
Preparation Time: 30 minutes
Ready Time: 4 hours

Ingredients:
- 2-3 lb pork tenderloin
- 2 tbsp olive oil
- 1.5 tsp smoked paprika
- Salt & pepper to taste
- 2 cups apple, diced
- 1/2 cup white onion, diced
- 2 tbsp apple cider vinegar
- 2 tsp coconut sugar
- 2 tbsp fresh parsley, chopped

Instructions:
1. Preheat your smoker or grill to 250°F

2. Rub olive oil, paprika, salt and pepper over the pork tenderloin, coating it fully
3. Place the pork in the smoker and cook for 3-3.5 hours until the internal temperature reaches 160°F
4. Meanwhile, prepare the apple chutney by combining apples, onion, apple cider vinegar, coconut sugar and parsley in a medium pot
5. Sauception over medium-low heat for 15 minutes, stirring occasionally, until the apples are tender
6. Once pork is cooked, let rest for a few minutes before slicing
7. Serve with apple chutney over top

Nutrition information: Calories: 187 kcal, Carbohydrates: 7 g, Protein: 27 g, Fat: 5 g, Saturated Fat: 1 g, Cholesterol: 79 mg, Sodium: 65 mg, Potassium: 459 mg, Fiber: 1 g, Sugar: 5 g, Vitamin A: 94 IU, Vitamin C: 3 mg, Calcium: 8 mg, Iron: 1 mg

45. Grilled Sweet Potato Wedges with Chipotle Mayo

Ready for a side dish that's looking for a party? Get ready to serve up grilled sweet potato wedges with a smoky chipotle mayo! This recipe is spicy, savory, salty, and a tad sweet. Enjoy with a glass of cold beer and your favorite dip!
Serving: 4-6
Preparation time: 15 minutes
Ready time: 25 minutes

Ingredients:
- 2 large sweet potatoes, peeled and cut into wedges
- 2 tablespoons olive oil
- Salt and pepper, to taste
- ¼ cup mayonnaise
- 2 teaspoons chipotle pepper sauce

Instructions:
1. Preheat grill to medium-high heat.
2. In a large bowl, toss together the sweet potato wedges with olive oil, salt, and pepper.

3. Place the sweet potato wedges onto a greased grill and cook for 10 minutes, flipping halfway through.
4. Meanwhile, in a small bowl whisk together the mayonnaise and chipotle pepper sauce until well combined.
5. Serve the grilled sweet potato wedges with chipotle mayo.

Nutrition information:
Amount Per Serving: Calories: 210 Total Fat: 10g Saturated Fat: 1.5g Trans Fat: 0g Cholesterol: 3mg Sodium: 177mg Carbohydrates: 28g Fiber: 3g Sugar: 6g Protein: 2g

46. Smoked Beef Brisket Burnt Ends

Smoked Beef Brisket Burnt Ends are the juicy and flavorful pieces of beef brisket that are baked in a smoker and then lightly coated in a sweet and savory glaze. They can be served as an appetizer or a main dish and are sure to impress guests at any event.
Serving: 10
Preparation Time: 10 minutes
Ready Time: 8-10 hours

Ingredients:
- 6-8 lb. Beef brisket
- 1 oz. Beef rub
- 1 oz. Worcestershire sauce
- 2 cups Barbecue sauce
- 2 cups of Wood chips

Instructions:
1. Prepare the beef brisket by rubbing it with the beef rub and Worcestershire sauce.
2. Place the beef brisket in a smoker and cover it with wood chips.
3. Smoker the beef brisket over a low flame for 8-10 hours.
4. Remove the brisket from the smoker and let cool before slicing.
5. Slice the brisket into 1-inch cubes and place them on a baking sheet.
6. Brush each cube with barbecue sauce.
7. Place the baking sheet in the oven or smoker and bake for 10 minutes.

8. Serve the smoked beef brisket burnt ends hot with additional barbecue sauce.

Nutrition information: Serving size 1, Calories 345, Total Fat 14g, Cholesterol 70mg, Sodium 640mg, Protein 22g, Total Carbohydrates 32g.

47. Grilled Caesar Salad with Grilled Chicken

Grilled Caesar salad is an easy, tasty and healthy dish. It's a great choice for a weeknight meal, or for entertaining. It starts with grilled chicken, topped with Caesar dressing, crispy bacon, and Parmesan cheese. The result is a light and flavorful salad that is sure to please.
Serving: 4
Preparation time: 10 minutes
Ready time: 25 minutes

Ingredients:
- 2 boneless, skinless chicken breasts
- 2 tablespoons olive oil
- Salt and freshly ground black pepper
- 2 tablespoons freshly squeezed lemon juice
- 4 cups romaine lettuce, cut into bite-sized pieces
- 4 slices bacon, cooked until crispy and diced
- 8 tablespoons Caesar dressing
- ¼ cup freshly grated Parmesan cheese

Instructions:
1. Preheat the oven to 400°F.
2. Rub the chicken breasts with the olive oil and season with salt and pepper.
3. Heat a grill pan over medium-high heat. Grill the chicken for 10 minutes, or until cooked through.
4. Place the lettuce in a bowl and add the lemon juice. Toss to combine.
5. Divide the lettuce among four plates. Slice the chicken and arrange on top of the lettuce.
6. Top with the bacon and 4 tablespoons of Caesar dressing per plate.
7. Sprinkle with Parmesan cheese.

Nutrition information:
Calories: 419, Fat: 23g, Carbohydrates: 12g, Protein: 32g, Cholesterol: 73mg, Sodium: 864mg

48. Smoked Tri-Tip with Chimichurri Sauce

This delicious smoked tri-tip steak is complimented with a delicious and zesty chimichurri sauce. It is sure to become a crowd favorite that can be served at any special occasion.
Serving: 4
Preparation Time: 25 minutes
Ready Time: 2-2.5 Hours

Ingredients:
- 1 (3-4 lb.) tri-tip
- 2 tablespoons olive oil
- Salt and pepper
- 2 cloves garlic
- 2 tablespoons chopped fresh oregano
- 1/2 cup red wine vinegar
- 1/4 cup finely chopped fresh parsley
- 1/4 cup finely chopped fresh cilantro
- 2 tablespoons lemon juice
- 1 tablespoon minced red jalapeño
- 1 teaspoon ground cumin
- 1/4 cup extra-virgin olive oil

Instructions:
1. Preheat smoker to 250° F.
2. Coat the tri-tip steak with olive oil and season liberally with salt and pepper.
3. Place the steak in the smoker and cook until it reaches an internal temperature of 135° F. (about 2-2.5 hours)
4. In a small bowl, combine the garlic, oregano, vinegar, parsley, cilantro, lemon juice, jalapeño, and cumin.
5. Drizzle in the olive oil and whisk to combine.
6. Let the chimichurri sauce sit for at least 10 minutes before serving.

7. Once the tri-tip is done cooking, allow it to rest for about 10 minutes before carving and serving with the chimichurri sauce.

Nutrition information:
Serving size: 4
Calories: 710
Total Fat: 40g
Saturated Fat: 11g
Cholesterol: 135mg
Sodium: 290mg
Carbohydrates: 2g
Fiber: 1g
Sugar: 0g
Protein: 78g

49. Grilled Peaches with Honey Mascarpone

This delicious dish of Grilled Peaches with Honey Mascarpone combines the freshness of peach with the creamy sweetness of honey mascarpone for a perfect end of summer treat.
Serving: 4
Preparation time: 10 minutes
Ready time: 15 minutes

Ingredients:
- 4 large ripe peaches, sliced in half
- 1 Tbsp olive oil
- 2 Tbsp honey
- 1/2 cup mascarpone cheese
- 2 Tbsp chopped pistachios
- 2 Tbsp mini chocolate chips
- Pinch of salt

Instructions:
1. Preheat your grill to medium-high heat.
2. Drizzle peach halves with olive oil, honey, and a pinch of salt.
3. Grill peaches for about 4 to 6 minutes.

4. Remove peaches from the grill and top each with a tablespoon of mascarpone cheese.
5. Sprinkle with chopped pistachios, mini chocolate chips, and a drizzle of honey.
6. Serve warm.

Nutrition information: Per serving: CAL 478, FAT 28.2g, CARB 49.8g, PRO 9.3g, FIB 4.2g, SUG 36.6g, CHOL 37.6mg, IRON 0.8mg, SODIUM 149.4mg

50. Smoked Turkey Legs with Maple Glaze

This Smoked Turkey Legs with Maple Glaze recipe is a flavorful and delicious way to prepare turkey. With its smoky and sweet flavor, this turkey recipe is sure to please!
Serving: 4-6
Preparation time: 10 minutes
Ready time: 4 hours

Ingredients:
- 4-6 turkey legs
- 2 cups of maple syrup
- 2 Tbsp of Worcestershire sauce
- 1/2 tsp garlic powder
- 2 tsp of smoked paprika
- Salt and pepper to taste

Instructions:
1. Preheat your smoker to 250 °F.
2. In a medium bowl, mix together maple syrup, Worcestershire sauce, garlic powder and smoked paprika.
3. Rub the mixture all over each turkey leg and season with salt and pepper.
4. Place the turkey legs in the smoker and smoke for 3-4 hours at 250 °F.
5. Once cooked, brush glaze over each leg and serve.

Nutrition information: by serving size (4-6 people); Calories: 416; Fat: 16.2g; Saturated Fat: 5.9g; Cholesterol: 188mg; Sodium: 228mg; Carbohydrates: 32.2g; Fiber: 0.3g; Protein: 33.1g.

51. Grilled Halloumi Salad with Lemon Vinaigrette

This light and fresh Grilled Halloumi Salad with Lemon Vinaigrette is a simple, healthy, and savory lunch or dinner that comes together quickly to please any crowd.
Serving: 6
Preparation Time: 15 minutes
Ready Time: 15 minutes

Ingredients:
- 250g halloumi cheese, cut into 2 cm thick slices
- 2 large tomatoes, chopped
- 1 red onion, finely chopped
- 2 lemons, juice and zest
- 2 tablespoons extra-virgin olive oil
- 2 tablespoons white balsamic vinegar
- 2 tablespoons honey
- Handful fresh basil leaves
- Salt and pepper to taste

Instructions:
1. Preheat a grill or a skillet over medium-high heat.
2. Arrange the halloumi slices on a plate and season with salt and pepper.
3. Grill or fry the halloumi slices until lightly charred and golden brown (about 2-3 minutes per side).
4. Place the grilled halloumi in a bowl with tomatoes and onion.
5. In a separate bowl, whisk together the lemon juice, zest, olive oil, balsamic vinegar, and honey.
6. Pour the dressing over the halloumi and vegetables, stirring to combine.
7. Add the basil leaves and toss to coat.
8. Season with salt and pepper, to taste.

Nutrition information (per serving):

- Calories: 253 kcal
- Fat: 17.1 g
- Carbohydrates: 16.1 g
- Protein: 13.8 g

52. Smoked Salmon Crostini with Herbed Cream Cheese

This Smoked Salmon Crostini with Herbed Cream Cheese is an easy appetizer that is ready in minutes. It's full of flavor and perfect for a party or your next gathering.
Serving: Makes 12 Crostini
Preparation Time: 10 minutes
Ready Time: 10 minutes

Ingredients:
　-12 thin slices of baguette, toasted
　-4 ounces cream cheese, softened
　-2 tablespoons fresh chives, chopped
　-2 tablespoons fresh dill, chopped
　-1/4 teaspoon garlic powder
　-1/4 teaspoon sea salt
　-2 teaspoons lemon juice
　-4 ounces smoked salmon

Instructions:
　1. Preheat your oven to 400 degrees F. Place the baguette slices on a baking sheet and bake for about 5 minutes or until lightly browned.
　2. In a small bowl, combine the cream cheese, chives, dill, garlic powder, sea salt and lemon juice and stir until combined.
　3. Spread the cream cheese mixture on top of each baguette slice and top with a slice of smoked salmon.
　4. Serve with the crostini.

Nutrition information: Calories: 44, Fat: 2.6g, Saturated fat: 1.1g, Carbohydrates: 3.5g, Sugar: 0.4g, Sodium: 212mg, Fiber: 0.4g, Protein: 3g

53. Grilled T-Bone Steak with Garlic Herb Butter

This Grilled T-Bone Steak with Garlic Herb Butter is a fast and flavor-filled meal that's sure to please the whole family. Perfectly grilled to your desired doneness, the steak is topped off with a garlic herb butter for an extra special touch.
Serving: 4
Preparation Time: 15 minutes
Ready Time: 15 minutes

Ingredients:
- 2 T-bone steaks
- 2 tablespoons olive oil
- Salt and pepper
- 2 tablespoons butter
- 2 cloves garlic, minced
- 2 tablespoons fresh herbs such as parsley, rosemary, thyme, and/or oregano

Instructions:
1. Preheat grill to medium-high heat.
2. Rub steaks with oil, salt, and pepper.
3. Grill steaks to desired doneness, about 6 minutes per side for medium-rare.
4. Meanwhile, in small saucepan, melt butter over medium heat.
5. Add garlic and herbs to melt butter, and simmer for 1 to 2 minutes.
6. Remove steaks from the grill and top with garlic herb butter.

Nutrition information (per serving):
Calories: 429, Fat: 19.7 g, Carbs: 0.6 g, Protein: 59.6 g

54. Smoked Pork Chops with Apple Bourbon Glaze

Smoked Pork Chops with Apple Bourbon Glaze is a delicious and easy to make recipe with juicy smoked pork chops, glazed in a sweet and smooth apple bourbon sauce. Enjoy this delightful dinner with your family and friends.

Serving: 4
Preparation time: 10 minutes
Ready time: 25 minutes

Ingredients:
4 boneless center-cut pork chops
2 tablespoons olive oil
1 teaspoon garlic powder
1 teaspoon smoked paprika
1/2 teaspoon black pepper
1/2 teaspoon salt
1 cup apple cider
1/4 cup bourbon
2 tablespoons unsalted butter
2 tablespoons brown sugar
1/2 teaspoon dried thyme

Instructions:
1. Preheat the smoker to 225°F.
2. Rub the pork chops with the olive oil, garlic powder, smoked paprika, pepper and salt.
3. Place the pork chops in the smoker and smoke for about 20 minutes, or until the internal temperature is 145°F.
4. Heat a small saucepan over medium-high heat. Add the apple cider and bourbon and simmer for 3 minutes.
5. Add the butter, brown sugar and thyme to the pan and simmer for 3-4 minutes, until the mixture is thick and syrupy.
6. Remove the pork chops from the smoker and brush them with the glaze. Serve.

Nutrition information:
Calories: 375
Fat: 20g
Carbohydrates: 8g
Protein: 39g

55. Grilled Vegetable Platter with Dips

Grilled Vegetable Platter with Dips is an easy and delicious dish to serve with appetizers or as a side to entrees. The grilling process adds a smoky flavor to the vegetables, enhancing their flavors, while the dips provide an extra zing. This recipe calls for six different vegetable items, but feel free to customize the platter with your favorite vegetables.
Serving: This recipe yields 6 servings.
Preparation time: 15 minutes
Ready time: 25 minutes

Ingredients:
- 2 bell peppers, sliced
- 2 ears of corn, cut in half
- 1 small eggplant, cubed
- 2 zucchini, sliced
- 2 carrots, sliced
- Olive oil
- Salt and pepper
- Your favorite dipping sauces (such as ranch, tzatziki, hummus, etc.)

Instructions:
1. Preheat the grill to medium-high heat.
2. Arrange the vegetables on a large sheet pan and toss with olive oil, salt, and pepper.
3. Place the vegetables on the preheated grill and cook, flipping occasionally, until lightly charred and cooked through, about 10 minutes.
4. Serve the vegetables with dipping sauces.

Nutrition information
Per Serving: Calories: 125 kcal
Carbohydrates: 15 g
Protein: 5 g
Fat: 5 g
Saturated Fat: 1 g
Sodium: 168 mg
Potassium: 646 mg
Fiber: 7 g
Sugar: 5 g

56. Smoked Meatloaf with BBQ Sauce

Smoked Meatloaf with BBQ Sauce is a delicious smoked meatloaf dish. Packed with flavor from a homemade BBQ sauce and a crisp, smoky outer crust, this family favorite is a great option for a weekday dinner or an easy summer cookout.

Serving: 6
Preparation time: 45 mins
Ready time: 2 hours

Ingredients:
- 1 lb ground beef
- ½ cup diced onion
- ¾ cup BBQ sauce, divided
- 1 egg, lightly beaten
- ½ cup breadcrumbs
- 1 tablespoon Worcestershire sauce
- 1 teaspoon garlic powder
- ½ teaspoon smoked paprika
- Salt and pepper, to taste

Instructions:
1. Preheat smoker to 250°F.
2. In a large bowl, combine ground beef, onion, ¼ cup BBQ sauce, egg, breadcrumbs, Worcestershire sauce, garlic powder, smoked paprika, and salt and pepper. Mix with your hands until well-combined.
3. Form into a loaf shape and place on a baking sheet, then transfer to the preheated smoker.
4. Smoke for 1 hour, then brush with remaining BBQ sauce.
5. Continue smoking for an additional hour, flipping the meatloaf midway through.
6. When done, a thermometer inserted into the center of the loaf should read 160°F.
7. Serve with additional BBQ sauce, if desired.

Nutrition information:
Serving size: 6 | Calories: 221 | Fat: 10 g | Saturated fat: 4 g | Cholesterol: 74 mg | Sodium: 314 mg | Carbohydrate: 13 g | Fiber: 1 g | Protein: 20 g

57. Grilled Octopus with Lemon Garlic Sauce

Enjoy this delicious warm weather favorite! Grilled Octopus with Lemon Garlic Sauce is full of flavor and a perfect meal option for summer cookouts.
Serving: Serves 4
Preparation Time: 15 minutes
Ready Time: 45 minutes

Ingredients:
- 3-4 lbs octopus
- 2 cloves garlic
- 1/4 cup olive oil
- Juice of 1 lemon
- 2 tablespoons chopped oregano
- Salt and pepper, to taste

Instructions:
1. Preheat the grill to high heat.
2. Clean and prepare the octopus by cutting into 2-inch slices.
3. Place the octopus in a bowl and season with garlic, olive oil, lemon juice, oregano, salt, and pepper, and mix to ensure the octopus is evenly coated.
4. Place the octopus slices onto the preheated grill and cook for 2 minutes on each side.
5. Serve with lemon garlic sauce on the side.

Nutrition information: Per serving: 280 calories, 21 g carbohydrate, 18.2 g fat, 16.4 g protein, 135 mg sodium, 4.3 g sugar.

58. Smoked Chicken and Sausage Jambalaya

Smoked Chicken and Sausage Jambalaya is a flavorful southern dish with smoky and savory aromas. The dish consists of chicken, sausage, vegetables, and rice cooked in a flavorful broth. It's a hearty meal that's sure to satisfy.
Serving: Serves 6-8.

Preparation time: 25 minutes
Ready time: 1 hour

Ingredients:
- 2 tablespoons of olive oil
- 1 yellow onion, chopped
- 2 cloves garlic, chopped
- 2 carrots, chopped
- 2 celery stalks, chopped
- 8 ounces of smoked sausage, sliced
- 1 pound of smoked chicken thighs, cut into bite-sized pieces
- 1 teaspoon smoked paprika
- 1 teaspoon thyme
- 2 teaspoons oregano
- 2 teaspoons salt
- 1/2 teaspoon black pepper
- 2 cups uncooked long grain white rice
- 4 cups chicken broth

Instructions:
1. Heat the olive oil in a large pot over medium heat.
2. Add the onion, garlic, carrots, and celery to the pot and stir to combine. Cook until the vegetables are softened, about 5 minutes.
3. Add the smoked sausage and chicken to the pot and cook for an additional 3-5 minutes until the chicken is just cooked through.
4. Add the smoked paprika, thyme, oregano, salt, pepper, and rice. Stir to combine all of the Ingredients.
5. Pour in the chicken broth. Bring the mixture to a boil, reduce to a simmer, cover, and cook for 20 minutes.
6. After 20 minutes, remove the pot from the heat and let it sit covered for 10 minutes.
7. Serve the jambalaya hot.

Nutrition information:
Each serving contains approximately 315 calories, 11g fat, 30g carbohydrates, and 17g protein.

59. Grilled Halloumi Skewers with Mediterranean Salsa

Enjoy a Mediterranean-inspired grilled halloumi skewer with freshly-made salsa. This easy-to-make appetizer is sure to tantalize any taste buds.
Serving: 4 skewers
Preparation time: 30 minutes
Ready time: 40 minutes

Ingredients:
- 8oz halloumi cheese, cut into bite-sized cubes
- 4 wooden skewers
- 3 ripe tomatoes
- 1 clove of garlic
- 1 red onion
- 1/4 cup of parsley
- 4 tablespoons of olive oil
- 2 tablespoons of red wine vinegar
- 1 lemon (juiced)
- Salt and pepper, to taste

Instructions:
1. Soak the wooden skewers in water for at least 15 minutes
2. Pre-heat the grill to medium-high heat
3. Peel and mince garlic
4. Cut tomato and red onion into small cubes
5. Place halloumi cubes onto the skewers
6. Grill the skewers for 5-7 minutes, flipping them every few minutes
7. Meanwhile, in a large bowl, mix together minced garlic, tomato, red onion, parsley, olive oil, red wine vinegar, lemon juice and season with salt and pepper
8. Remove the skewers from the grill and serve with the salsa

Nutrition information:
Calories: 320 kcal
Total Fat: 18.3g
Sodium: 533mg
Carbohydrates: 10.6g

Protein: 22.8g

60. Smoked Stuffed Bell Peppers

This delicious Smoked Stuffed Bell Peppers recipe is easy to make and can be customized for any palette. Its unique combination of flavorful Ingredients creates an unforgettable and unique meal that is sure to please.
Serving: 4
Preparation Time: 10 min
Ready Time: 45 min

Ingredients:
- 4 large bell peppers
- 1/2 cup cooked and crumbled sausage
- 1 cup black beans, cooked and drained
- 1/2 cup cooked white rice
- 1/2 red onion, finely diced
- 1 teaspoon smoked paprika
- 1 teaspoon garlic powder
- 1/2 teaspoon chili powder
- 1/4 teaspoon cumin
- Salt and pepper to taste
- 1/2 cup grated cheese
- 1/4 cup tomato sauce

Instructions:
1. Preheat your smoker or grill to 225 degrees.
2. Cut the tops off the bell peppers and remove the seeds.
3. In a large bowl, combine the sausage, black beans, cooked rice, diced onion, smoked paprika, garlic powder, chili powder, cumin, salt, and pepper. Mix well.
4. Spoon the sausage mixture into the bell peppers, filling each one evenly.
5. Place the stuffed peppers on the preheated smoker or grill. Smoke for 30 minutes.
6. After 30 minutes, remove the peppers from the smoker or grill and top each one with grated cheese. Return to the smoker or grill and

smoke for an additional 15 minutes or until the cheese is melted and bubbly.
7. Remove from heat and serve immediately with tomato sauce.

Nutrition information:
- Calories: 337
- Fat: 10g
- Protein: 16g
- Carbs: 47g
- Sodium: 408mg

61. Grilled Lemon Herb Chicken Wings

Grilled Lemon Herb Chicken Wings are a flavorful, zesty meal that will tantalize your taste buds. This dish is easy to make and is perfect for picnics, barbecues, or a romantic dinner.
Serving: 3-4 servings
Preparation time: 15 minutes
Ready time: 35 minutes

Ingredients:
- 8 chicken wings
- 2 tablespoons olive oil
- 2 tablespoons lemon juice
- 2 tablespoons fresh oregano, finely chopped
- 1 teaspoon garlic powder
- 1/2 teaspoon chili powder
- 1/2 teaspoon garlic salt
- Salt and pepper to taste

Instructions:
1. Preheat an outdoor grill to medium-high heat.
2. In a small bowl, combine the olive oil, lemon juice, oregano, garlic powder, chili powder, garlic salt, salt, and pepper.
3. Rub the marinade over the chicken wings.
4. Place chicken wings on preheated grill and cook for 25 minutes or until cooked through.
5. Serve the grilled chicken wings with your favorite sides.

Nutrition information:
Serving size: 1/4 of recipe
Calories: 208 kcal
Total Fat: 11.8 g
Saturated Fat: 3.0 g
Cholesterol: 66 mg
Sodium: 367 mg
Carbohydrates: 0.8 g
Protein: 22.5 g

62. Smoked Beef Short Ribs with Red Wine Glaze

Tender and juicy, these smoked beef short ribs with a savory redwine glaze are sure to be a hit at your next special occasion or family get together.
Serving: 12
Preparation time: 10 minutes
Ready time: 4-6 hours

Ingredients:
- 5-6lbs Beef Short Ribs
- 2 cups BBQ Rub/Seasoning
- 2 cups Hardwood Pellets (mesquite)
- 2 cups Red Wine
- 2 cups Beef Stock
- 1/2 cup Worcestershire Sauce
- 1/2 cup Balsamic Vinegar
- 1/2 cup Brown Sugar
- 1/4 cup Olive Oil

Instructions:
1. Preheat smoker to 225°F.
2. Place short ribs on a large baking sheet. Sprinkle liberally with your favorite BBQ rub/seasoning.
3. Place wood pellets in the smoker. Place seasoned ribs inside the smoker and cook for 4-6 hours.

4. In a medium-sized saucepan, heat the red wine, beef stock, Worcestershire sauce, balsamic vinegar, and brown sugar over medium heat. Bring to a slow simmer for 10 minutes, stirring occasionally, until the liquid has reduced by half.
5. Remove ribs from heat and brush with the red wine glaze. Bake for an additional 10 minutes to develop deeper flavor.
6. Serve and enjoy.

Nutrition information: Per serving (based on 6 servings): 996 calories, 81.1 g fat, 5.3 g carbohydrates, 53.5 g protein

63. Grilled Shrimp and Pineapple Skewers with Teriyaki Glaze

Grilled Shrimp and Pineapple Skewers with Teriyaki Glaze is a delicious and healthy dish perfect for summer barbecues. This vibrant combination of succulent shrimp and juicy pineapple is glazed in a sweet and savory teriyaki sauce, creating an appetizing flavor combination and a stunning presentation.
Serving: 4-6
Preparation Time: 15 minutes
Ready Time: 20 minutes

Ingredients:
- 12 jumbo shrimp, peeled and deveined
- 2 cups fresh pineapple, cubed
- 1/3 cup teriyaki sauce
- 1 tablespoon vegetable oil
- Salt and black pepper, to taste

Instructions:
1. Preheat the grill to medium-high heat.
2. Thread the shrimp and pineapple cubes onto individual skewers.
3. In a small bowl, whisk together the teriyaki sauce, vegetable oil, salt, and black pepper.
4. Brush the teriyaki glaze onto the skewered Ingredients.
5. Place the skewers onto the preheated grill and cook for 3-4 minutes per side, or until the shrimp is cooked through.

6. Serve immediately.

Nutrition information:
Calories: 111, Fat: 4 g, Cholesterol: 115 mg, Sodium: 293 mg, Carbohydrates: 11 g, Protein: 9 g, Potassium: 176 mg

64. Smoked Lamb Burgers with Tzatziki Sauce

This delicious recipe from Mediterranean cuisine combines juicy, flavorful lamb burgers with cool and creamy Tzatziki sauce.
Serving: Makes 4 servings
Preparation Time: 10 minutes
Ready Time: 15 minutes

Ingredients:
- 1lb Ground Lamb
- 2 cloves of Garlic, minced
- 1tsp Dried Oregano
- 1 tsp Ground Cumin
- Salt and Pepper, to taste
- 1/2cup Plain Greek Yogurt
- 1 Cucumber, seeded and diced
- 2tbsp Fresh Dill, chopped
- 2tbsp Olive Oil

Instructions:
1. Preheat a grill to medium-high heat.
2. In a large bowl, combine the lamb, garlic, oregano, cumin, and salt and pepper. Form into 4 burgers.
3. Grill burgers for about 5 minutes per side or until cooked to desired doneness.
4. To make the tzatziki sauce, combine the yogurt, cucumber, dill, and olive oil. Mix until well combined.
5. Serve burgers with tzatziki sauce on the side.

Nutrition information:
- Calories: 275
- Protein: 16g

- Fat: 19g
- Carbohydrates: 8g
- Fiber: 0.5g

65. Grilled Zucchini Rolls with Goat Cheese and Sun-Dried Tomatoes

Grilled Zucchini Rolls with Goat Cheese and Sun-Dried Tomatoes is an easy to make appetizer full of flavor and color!
Serving: 4
Preparation time: 10 mins
Ready time: 8 mins

Ingredients:
- 2 large zucchinis
- 1/3 cup goat cheese
- 1/4 cup chopped sun-dried tomatoes
- 2 tablespoons olive oil
- Salt and pepper to taste

Instructions:
1. Preheat the grill to medium-high heat.
2. Slice the zucchini into long thin strips.
3. In a medium bowl, mix together the goat cheese, sun-dried tomatoes, olive oil and salt and pepper.
4. Spread the goat cheese mixture onto each strip of zucchini.
5. Roll each strip of zucchini and secure with a toothpick.
6. Grill the rolls for 8 minutes or until lightly golden brown and slightly crispy.

Nutrition information: serving size: 4, calories: 144, total fat: 10g, saturated fat: 4g, cholesterol: 15mg, sodium: 141mg, carbohydrate: 7g, dietary fiber: 2g, sugars: 4g, protein: 6g.

66. Smoked Chicken Fajitas with Peppers and Onions

This is a delectable meal of smoky chicken fajitas with grilled peppers and onions. Perfect for a weeknight meal, this meal is easy to make, and tastes amazing.
Serving: 4
Preparation Time: 10 minutes
Ready Time: 20 minutes

Ingredients:
- 2 boneless chicken breasts, cut into strips
- 2 bell peppers (red or green), thinly sliced
- 1 onion, finely diced
- 2 tablespoons olive oil
- 1/2 teaspoon smoked paprika
- Salt and pepper
- 4-6 tortillas

Instructions:
1. Preheat a grill or grill pan to medium-high.
2. Place the chicken strips in a bowl and season with the smoked paprika, salt, and pepper.
3. Drizzle the peppers and onions with the olive oil and season with salt and pepper.
4. Place the chicken strips and the peppers and onions onto the preheated pan.
5. Grill for 8-10 minutes, or until the chicken is cooked through.
6. Place the cooked chicken and vegetables onto the tortillas and serve with your favorite toppings.

Nutrition information:
Calories: 320; Fat: 14g; Carbs: 25g; Protein: 21g

67. Grilled Steak Fajitas with Salsa and Guacamole

Enjoy the classic flavor of steak fajitas with a delicious salsa and guacamole toppings! This classic Mexican dish is sure to please everyone in the family.
Serving: Serves 4
Preparation Time: 10 minutes

Ready Time: 20 minutes

Ingredients:
- 1 lb sliced steak
- 4-5 soft flour tortillas
- 1 red bell pepper, sliced
- 1 red onion, sliced
- 2 cloves garlic, minced
- 2 tablespoons olive oil
- 2 teaspoons Mexican seasoning
- 1/2 cup salsa
- 1/2 cup guacamole
- 2 tablespoons cilantro, chopped

Instructions:
1. Preheat the grill to medium high heat.
2. In a large bowl, mix together the steak, bell pepper, red onion, and garlic.
3. Add the olive oil and Mexican seasoning and mix together until everything is evenly coated.
4. Place the steak mixture onto the preheated grill and cook for 8-10 minutes.
5. While the steak is cooking, warm the tortillas in the microwave.
6. Once the steak is cooked through, assemble the fajitas by placing the steak mixture onto the tortillas.
7. Add the salsa and guacamole to the top of the steak and top with the chopped cilantro.
8. Serve immediately and enjoy!

Nutrition information (per serving):
Calories: 411 Protein: 28g Fat: 20g Carbs: 25g

68. Smoked Pork Loin with Apple Cider Glaze

This Smoked Pork Loin with Apple Cider Glaze is a savory and juicy smoked recipe that is sure to impress your family and friends.
Serving: 8-10
Preparation time: 10 minutes

Ready time: 2 hours

Ingredients:
- 2 lbs boneless pork loin
- 2 cloves garlic, minced
- 2 tablespoons fresh thyme
- 2 tablespoons olive oil
- 2 teaspoons cider vinegar
- 2 tablespoons honey
- 1 tablespoon mustard

Instructions:
1. Preheat the smoker to 225F.
2. In a small bowl, combine the garlic, thyme, olive oil, cider vinegar, honey, and mustard.
3. Rub this mixture over the pork loin and place it in the smoker.
4. Cook for about 2 hours or until the internal temperature of the pork loin reaches 145F.
5. Remove the pork loin from the smoker and let it rest for 10-15 minutes before slicing.
6. Drizzle the pork loin with the Apple Cider Glaze and enjoy.

Nutrition information: Per Serving: Calories 285, Total Fat 9.2g, Cholesterol 95.1mg, Sodium 247mg, Total Carbohydrates 8.8g, Protein 36.4g

69. Grilled Halloumi Burger with Roasted Red Pepper Sauce

Grilled Halloumi Burger with Roasted Red Pepper Sauce is a delicious and easy vegan burger which is flavoured with creamy roasted red pepper sauce. It is a healthy and filling meal that is sure to satisfy anyone's cravings.
Serving: 4
Preparation Time: 10 minutes
Ready Time: 25 minutes

Ingredients:

- 8 ounce of Halloumi cheese, cubed
- 2 red bell peppers
- 4 burger buns
- 1 large onion, chopped
- 2 tablespoons olive oil
- 2 cloves of garlic, minced
- 1 teaspoon smoked paprika
- 1/2 teaspoon sea salt
- 1/4 teaspoon black pepper

For the Red Pepper Sauce:
- 2 red bell peppers, roasted and seeded
- 1 garlic clove, minced
- 1 tablespoon olive oil
- 1/4 cup plain Greek yogurt
- 1 tablespoon fresh lemon juice
- Salt and pepper, to taste

Instructions:
1. Preheat your oven to 375 degrees and lightly grease a baking sheet. Place the cubed Halloumi on the baking sheet along with the bell peppers and onion. Drizzle olive oil over the vegetables, and make sure the Halloumi is evenly coated.
2. Roast the vegetables for about 20 minutes or until they are lightly browned. Once they're finished, remove them from the oven and let them cool.
3. Meanwhile, make the red pepper sauce. Place the bell peppers in a food processor along with the garlic, olive oil, yogurt, and lemon juice. Process until the mixture is smooth and season with salt and pepper, to taste.
4. To assemble the burgers, lightly toast the buns and place the Halloumi on each. Top with a spoonful of roasted vegetables and a generous amount of red pepper sauce. Serve immediately.

Nutrition information:
Calories: 285 kcal, Carbohydrates: 30 g, Protein: 14 g, Fat: 15 g, Saturated Fat: 8 g, Cholesterol: 28 mg, Sodium: 594 mg, Potassium: 170 mg, Fiber: 4 g, Sugar: 6 g, Vitamin A: 1850 IU, Vitamin C: 60.8 mg, Calcium: 214 mg, Iron: 2.2 mg

70. Smoked Stuffed Mushrooms with Cream Cheese and Bacon

These smoked stuffed mushrooms are stuffed with a delicious mix of cream cheese and bacon that balance perfectly for an easy appetizer or snack.
Serving: Makes 8
Preparation Time: 10 minutes
Ready Time: 1 hour

Ingredients:
- 8 large mushrooms
- 1/4 cup cream cheese
- 2 strips of cooked bacon, crumbled
- Few drops liquid smoke

Instructions:
1. Preheat the oven to 375 degrees F.
2. Carefully remove the stems from the mushrooms.
3. In a bowl, mix together the cream cheese, bacon and liquid smoke until combined.
4. Stuff each mushroom with the cream cheese mixture.
5. Place the stuffed mushrooms on a baking sheet and bake for 20 minutes.

Nutrition information: Calories: 146, Fat: 11.5g, Sodium: 104mg, Sugar: 1g, Carbohydrates: 4.9g, Protein: 5.7g

71. Grilled Herb-Marinated Tofu Skewers

A delicious vegetarian entrée, these Grilled Herb-Marinated Tofu Skewers are easy to make and composed of a tantalizing blend of savory Ingredients that will make your taste buds happy.
Serving: 4-6
Preparation time: 1 hour
Ready Time
2 hours

Ingredients:
- 14 oz. extra-firm tofu
- 2 tablespoons olive oil
- 2 tablespoons fresh grated ginger
- 1/4 cup lime juice
- 1/4 cup honey
- 2-3 cloves garlic, minced
- 2 tablespoons tamari soy sauce
- 2 tablespoons vegan worcestershire sauce
- 1 tablespoon fresh thyme, minced
- 1 tablespoon rosemary, minced
- Salt and pepper to taste

Instructions:
1. Press the tofu for at least 1 hour and preheat the grill to medium heat.
2. In a small bowl, combine the olive oil, ginger, lime juice, honey, garlic, tamari soy sauce, vegan worcestershire sauce, thyme, rosemary, salt, and pepper.
3. Cut the tofu into cubes and place them into a large bowl.
4. Pour the marinade over the tofu and gently toss to combine.
5. Cover the bowl and refrigerate for at least 1 hour.
6. Thread the cubes of tofu onto skewers and place them on the preheated grill.
7. Grill for 4-6 minutes on each side or until lightly browned and slightly charred.
8. Serve and enjoy!

Nutrition information
Calories: 133
Fat: 7g
Carbohydrates: 11g
Protein: 7g
Sodium: 582mg

72. Smoked Cornish Hens with Herb Butter

This recipe for smoked cornish hens with herb butter is a flavorful and succulent dish. The salty smokiness of the birds, combined with the

sweetness of the herb butter, creates an amazing flavor profile that will tantalize your taste buds.
Serving: This recipe serves 4 people.
Preparation Time: 15 minutes
Ready Time: 1 hour and 15 minutes

Ingredients:
- 4 Cornish hens, cleaned, giblets and neck removed
- 2 tablespoons smoked sea salt
- 2 tablespoons chili powder
- 2 tablespoons garlic powder
- 2 tablespoons onion powder
- 3 tablespoons olive oil
- 1 tablespoon Italian seasoning
- 1/2 cup butter, softened
- 2 cloves garlic, minced
- 2 teaspoons fresh thyme, chopped
- 2 teaspoons fresh rosemary, chopped
- 2 teaspoons fresh parsley, chopped
- Salt and freshly cracked black pepper, to taste

Instructions:
1. Preheat a smoker to 225^0F.
2. Clean and dry the hens and remove the giblets. Place the hens in a large bowl and rub with the smoked salt, chili powder, garlic powder, onion powder, and olive oil. Place the hens in the smoker and close the lid. Smoke for 1 hour or until the internal temperature of the hens reaches 165^0F.
3. In a small bowl, cream together the butter, garlic, thyme, rosemary, and parsley.
4. Coat the hens with the herb butter mixture and season with salt and pepper. Increase the temperature of the smoker to 300^0F and cook for an additional 15 minutes, or until the internal temperature of the hens reaches 165^0F.
5. Serve the hens with the remaining herb butter and enjoy.

Nutrition information: Per serving: 748 calories, 49g fat, 68g protein, 5g carbohydrates, 2.3g fiber.

73. Grilled Teriyaki Salmon with Sesame Seeds

Start your meal with a healthy and delicious grilled teriyaki salmon with sesame seeds! This dish is flavored with a soy, ginger, garlic and brown sugar marinade to provide a juicy and flavorful meal.
Serving: Serves 4
Preparation time: 10 minutes
Ready time: 15 minutes

Ingredients:
- 4x4 ounce salmon fillets
- 2 tablespoons soy sauce
- 1 tablespoon rice vinegar
- 1 tablespoon brown sugar
- 1/2 teaspoon garlic powder
- 1/2 teaspoon ground ginger
- 2 teaspoons sesame oil
- 2 tablespoons sesame seeds

Instructions:
1. In a small bowl, mix together the soy sauce, rice vinegar, brown sugar, garlic powder and ground ginger.
2. Place the salmon fillets in a shallow dish and pour over the marinade. Cover and let the salmon marinate for 5 minutes.
3. Preheat the grill to medium-high heat and lightly oil the grate.
4. Place the salmon fillets on the grill and brush with the remaining marinade. Close the lid and let the salmon cook for 3 minutes.
5. Flip the salmon and brush with the remaining marinade. Close the lid and cook for another 3 minutes.
6. Remove the salmon from the grill and sprinkle with sesame oil and sesame seeds.

Nutrition information: Calories: 320, Fat: 16 g, Saturated fat: 3.5 g, Carbohydrates: 12 g, Protein: 34 g

74. Smoked Meatballs with Tangy BBQ Sauce

Smoked Meatballs with Tangy BBQ Sauce is an easy and flavorful meal packed with seasoned beef, smoked bacon, and delicious BBQ sauce.
Serving: 6-8
Preparation time: 10 minutes
Ready time: 35 minutes

Ingredients:
- 1 lb lean ground beef
- ½ lb bacon
- ½ cup diced white onions
- 1 teaspoon garlic powder
- 1 teaspoon smoked paprika
- ¼ cup BBQ Sauce

Instructions:
1. Preheat the oven to 400° F
2. In a large bowl, combine the beef, bacon, onions, garlic power, and smoked paprika. Form into 1-inch meatballs and place them onto a baking sheet lined with parchment paper.
3. Bake for 25 minutes.
4. In a separate bowl, mix together the BBQ Sauce. After the 25 minutes of baking, coat each meatball with the BBQ sauce.
5. Return to the oven and bake for an additional 10 minutes.

Nutrition information: Calories: 214, Fat: 16g, Carbs: 4g, Protein: 14g.

75. Grilled Shrimp Po' Boy Sandwiches with Remoulade Sauce

This Grilled Shrimp Po' Boy Sandwiches with Remoulade Sauce are easy to make and can be a great dinner or lunch option. It is a classic Louisiana sandwich made with hot and juicy fried shrimp.
Serving: 4
Preparation time: 20 minutes
Ready time: 50 minutes

Ingredients:

- 18 extra jumbo shrimp, peeled and deveined
- ¼ cup of olive oil
- Salt and ground black pepper, to taste
- 2 tablespoons of lemon juice
- 4 (4-ounce) beefsteak tomatoes, sliced
- 4 hamburger buns
- 2 heads of butter lettuce
- 2 tablespoons of mayonnaise
- Remoulade Sauce
- 1½ cups of ketchup
- 2 tablespoons of yellow mustard
- 1 tablespoon of paprika
- 2 cloves of garlic, minced
- 2 tablespoons of prepared horseradish
- 2 tablespoons of apple cider vinegar
- 2 tablespoons of Worcestershire sauce
- 2 tablespoons of freshly chopped parsley
- 2 tablespoons of chopped green onions

Instructions:
1. Preheat the grill to high heat.
2. In a medium bowl, add the shrimp, olive oil, salt, pepper, and lemon juice and toss to combine.
3. Place the shrimp on the grill and cook for 4 minutes, flipping once.
4. To assemble the sandwich, place a slice of tomato on each bun, top with lettuce, and place the grilled shrimp.
5. Combine the mayonnaise and Remoulade sauce and spread evenly across the top buns.
6. Make the Remoulade sauce by combining the ketchup, mustard, paprika, garlic, horseradish, vinegar, Worcestershire sauce, parsley, and green onions in a bowl.
7. Serve the sandwiches with the Remoulade sauce and enjoy.

Nutrition information:
Calories: 440, Fat: 22g, Carbohydrates: 31g, Protein: 28g, Sodium: 990mg, Fibre: 5g, Sugar: 10g.

76. Smoked Chicken Enchiladas with Green Chile Sauce

This recipe for Smoked Chicken Enchiladas with Green Chile Sauce is a delicious take on a classic Mexican dish! It's made with a flavorful tomato and green chile-based enchilada sauce, as well as zesty smoked chicken. The result is a mouthwatering combination that is sure to be a hit with the whole family!

Serving: 4
Preparation Time: 25 minutes
Ready Time: 45 minutes

Ingredients:
- 1 tablespoon olive oil
- 1 onion, diced
- 1 red bell pepper, diced
- 1 teaspoon ground cumin
- 1 teaspoon chili powder
- 1 teaspoon garlic powder
- 1 teaspoon dried oregano
- 1 (15-ounce) can of diced tomato
- 1 (4-ounce) can of diced green chiles
- 1 (14-ounce) can of tomato sauce
- 8 (6-inch) flour tortillas
- 2 cups of shredded smoked chicken
- 2 cups of shredded cheese
- Shredded lettuce and sliced avocados for topping (optional)

Instructions:
1. Preheat the oven to 375 degrees Fahrenheit.
2. In a large skillet over medium-high heat, heat the olive oil. Add the onions and bell peppers and sauté for 5 minutes.
3. Add the cumin, chili powder, garlic powder, and oregano, and cook for an additional 2 minutes.
4. Stir in the diced tomato, diced green chiles, and tomato sauce. Simmer for 10 minutes.
5. Place the tortillas on a work surface. Divide the smoked chicken, shredded cheese, and sauce evenly among the tortillas. Roll up the tortillas and place in a baking dish.

6. Pour the remaining sauce over the enchiladas. Top with the remaining cheese.
7. Bake for 25 minutes or until the cheese is melted and bubbling.
8. Serve the enchiladas topped with lettuce and avocados, if desired.

Nutrition information: Per Serving (1 enchilada):
Calories: 431; Fat: 16g; Carbohydrates: 44g; Protein: 27g; Sodium: 1178mg; Fiber: 5g; Sugar: 10g.

77. Grilled Artichokes with Lemon Garlic Aioli

Grilled Artichokes with Lemon Garlic Aioli is a simple and delicious appetizer. The earthy flavor of the artichoke hearts is complemented by a creamy and zesty garlic aioli, giving the dish a perfect balance between savory and creamy.
Serving: 2
Preparation Time: 10 minutes
Ready Time: 25 minutes

Ingredients:
- 2 artichokes
- 2 tablespoons olive oil
- Juice of 1 lemon
- 2 cloves garlic, minced
- ½ cup mayonnaise
- Salt and pepper to taste

Instructions:
1. Preheat grill to medium-high heat.
2. Cut off the artichokes' stems and remove the tough outer leaves. Cut each artichoke in half and place on a cutting board.
3. Drizzle olive oil on artichoke halves and place them cut-side down on the preheated grill. Grill for about 10 minutes, until the leaves are slightly charred.
4. Meanwhile, whisk together the lemon juice, garlic, mayonnaise, salt, and pepper until a creamy aioli is formed.
5. Serve artichokes warm with the lemon garlic aioli.

Nutrition information: Serving size: 1 artichoke half with aioli: Calories: 200, Total fat: 16g, Saturated fat: 2g, Cholesterol: 5mg, Sodium: 300mg, Carbohydrate: 10g, Fiber: 5g, Protein: 3g.

78. Smoked Beef Kabobs with Garlic Herb Marinade

Smoked Beef Kabobs with Garlic Herb Marinade is an easy and flavorful kabob option perfect for the grill. Marinated overnight, these kabobs are filled with juicy pieces of steak and vegetables that will tantalize everyone's taste buds!
Serving: Makes 4 Servings
Preparation time: Overnight marination
Ready time: 20 minutes

Ingredients:
- 1 lb flank steak, cut into 1" cubes
- 2 tablespoons olive oil
- 2 tablespoons lemon juice
- 1 tablespoon Worcestershire sauce
- 1 tablespoon chopped garlic
- 1 teaspoon ground black pepper
- 2 teaspoons dried oregano
- 1 teaspoon dried basil
- 1 teaspoon garlic powder
- 2 teaspoons course salt
- 1 red bell pepper, cut into 1" cubes
- 1 yellow bell pepper, cut into 1" cubes
- 2 zucchini, cut into 1" cubes
- 1 onion, cut into 1" cubes

Instructions:
1. In a medium bowl, whisk together olive oil, lemon juice, Worcestershire sauce, garlic, black pepper, oregano, basil, garlic powder, and salt.
2. Place steak cubes into the mixture and mix to make sure all pieces are coated. Cover the bowl and let sit overnight in the refrigerator.
3. Soak wooden skewers in water for at least 30 minutes prior to assembling kabobs.

4. Prepare the vegetables and thread onto the skewers, alternating between pieces of steak and vegetables.
5. Preheat an outdoor grill for medium heat.
6. Brush the grill with some oil to prevent sticking and place the kabobs on the grill.
7. Grill for 10-15 minutes, turning occasionally, until the steak and vegetables have reached desired doneness.

Nutrition information (Per Serving):
Calories: 325
Total Fat: 9g
Saturated Fat: 3g
Cholesterol: 76mg
Sodium: 598mg
Carbohydrates: 17g
Fiber: 4g
Sugar: 6g
Protein: 37g

79. Grilled Portobello Burger with Avocado and Pesto

Serve up something special with this mouthwatering Grilled Portobello Burger with Avocado and Pesto. Rich and creamy with just the right amount of zest, these burgers are full of flavor and texture.
Serving: 4
Preparation Time: 15 minutes
Ready Time: 20 minutes

Ingredients:
- 4 large portobello mushrooms
- 2 teaspoons olive oil
- Salt and freshly ground black pepper, to taste
- 2 avocados, sliced
- ½ cup basil pesto
- 4 hamburger buns, split

Instructions:

1. Preheat an outdoor grill to medium-high heat.
2. Brush the mushrooms with olive oil and season with salt and pepper.
3. Grill the mushrooms for 4-5 minutes per side, until lightly charred and heated through.
4. Spread pesto on the buns and top with mushrooms.
5. Top the mushrooms with avocado slices, close the burgers and serve.

Nutrition information:
Calories: 251.8, Total Fat: 12.7 g, Saturated Fat: 2.3 g, Cholesterol: 0 mg, Sodium: 253.7 mg, Carbohydrates: 26.3 g, Dietary Fiber: 7.3 g, Sugar: 5.4 g, Protein: 7.3 g.

80. Smoked Turkey Burgers with Cranberry Mayo

Smoked Turkey Burgers with Cranberry Mayo are hearty burgers that have plenty of fresh flavor thanks to the cranberry mayo and smoked turkey.
Serving: 4
Preparation Time: 20 minutes
Ready Time: 20 minutes

Ingredients:
- 4 smoked turkey burgers
- ½ cup mayonnaise
- ½ cup cranberry sauce
- lettuce and tomato, if desired

Instructions:
1. Preheat a skillet or grill over medium heat.
2. Place the burgers on the skillet/grill and cook for 5 minutes per side.
3. In a small bowl, combine the mayo and cranberry sauce. Mix until fully combined.
4. Once the burgers are cooked through, assemble the burgers with a dollop of the cranberry mayo, lettuce, and tomato.
5. Serve and enjoy.

Nutrition information:

Calories: 290Kcal, Total fat: 16g, Saturated fat: 2g, Cholesterol: 95mg, Sodium: 132mg, Total carbohydrate: 10g, Dietary fiber: 0g, Sugar: 10g, Protein: 25g

81. Grilled Veggie Quesadillas with Guacamole

Grilled Veggie Quesadilla with Guacamole is a delicious and flavorful vegetarian Mexican dish, sure to please the entire family. It is a great meal idea that is easy to make and sure to impress.
Serving: 4
Preparation time: 10 minutes
Ready time: 15 minutes

Ingredients:
- 2 large flour or wheat tortillas
- 2 cups cooked mixed vegetables (corn, bell peppers, zucchini, mushrooms, etc.)
- 1/2 cup shredded cheese
- 2 tablespoons olive oil
- 1/2 cup freshly prepared guacamole
- Salt and pepper to taste

Instructions:
1. Preheat a large skillet over medium heat.
2. Brush each tortilla with olive oil and place oiled side down in the preheated skillet.
3. Sprinkle half the shredded cheese, followed by half of the cooked vegetables over the tortilla.
4. Once the cheese has melted, fold the tortilla in half and press down lightly to form a quesadilla.
5. Grill each quesadilla for 2-3 minutes per side, until the outside is crisp and golden brown.
6. Carefully remove quesadillas from the skillet and place on a cutting board.
7. Allow quesadillas to cool slightly, then slice into wedges.
8. Serve with freshly prepared guacamole and enjoy.

Nutrition information:

Per serving (1 quesadilla wedge): Calories 250, Total fat 10g, Saturated fat 3g, Cholesterol 15 mg, Sodium 300 mg, Total carbohydrates 29 g, Dietary fiber 3 g, Sugars 3 g, Protein 8 g.

82. Smoked Stuffed Jalapeños with Cream Cheese and Bacon

Get smoky, cheesy, and bacon flavors all in one mouthful with these delightfully crunchy and delicious Smoked Stuffed Jalapeños with Cream Cheese and Bacon.
Serving: 8 stuffed jalapeños
Preparation time: 12 minutes
Ready time: 30 minutes

Ingredients:
- 8 jalapeno peppers
- 4 ounces cream cheese, softened
- 8 slices of bacon, cooked and crumbled
- Optional: 2 tablespoons chopped fresh chives

Instructions:
1. Preheat an outdoor smoker to 225 degrees F.
2. Slice the jalapeños in half and scoop out the seeds.
3. Fill the jalapeños with cream cheese and top with bacon crumbles.
4. Place the jalapeño halves on the smoker rack.
5. Smoke the jalapeños for 18 minutes.
6. Plate the jalapeños and sprinkle with chives.

Nutrition information:
Calories: 153; Total Fat: 15 g; Saturated Fat: 6 g; Trans Fat: 0 g; Cholesterol: 30 mg; Sodium: 292 mg; Carbohydrates: 2 g; Fiber: 1 g; Sugars: 1 g; Protein: 2 g

83. Grilled Lemon Herb Swordfish Steaks

Grilled Lemon Herb Swordfish Steaks is a light and flavorful meal that can be prepared in just a few minutes. This dish is a great way to enjoy swordfish, combining the bright tastes of lemon and herbs.

Serving: 4
Preparation time: 10 minutes
Ready time: 10 minutes

Ingredients:
- 4 swordfish steaks (6 ounces each)
- 4 tablespoons extra-virgin olive oil
- 2 tablespoons freshly squeezed lemon juice
- 2 teaspoons dried oregano
- 1 teaspoon dried thyme
- 1/2 teaspoon paprika
- 1/2 teaspoon black pepper
- Salt, to taste

Instructions:
1. Preheat the grill to medium-high heat.
2. In a medium bowl, whisk together the olive oil, lemon juice, oregano, thyme, paprika, black pepper, and salt.
3. Place the swordfish steaks in the bowl and turn to coat on all sides with the oil-lemon-herb mixture.
4. Grill the steaks for 3-4 minutes per side, or until the fish is just cooked through.
5. Serve the swordfish steaks with extra lemon wedges as desired.

Nutrition information: Per serving (6 ounces):
- Calories: 260
- Fat: 16g
- Carbohydrates: 1g
- Protein: 30g

84. Smoked Baby Back Ribs with Coffee Rub

Enjoy the savory flavors of smoked baby back ribs with a unique coffee rub. This recipe creates a delicious BBQ flavor that your guests won't soon forget.

Serving: 6 servings
Preparation Time: 2 hours
Ready Time: 5 hours

Ingredients:
- 2 racks baby back ribs
- 2 cups coffee grounds
- 1/4 cup brown sugar
- 2 tablespoons celery salt
- 2 teaspoons garlic salt
- 2 teaspoons smoked paprika
- 2 teaspoons freshly ground black pepper

Instructions:
1. Preheat smoker to 225°F
2. Combine all Ingredients to make the rub and mix well
3. Rub ribs on both sides with the rub
4. Place ribs on the smoker and cook for 3-4 hours until the ribs reach an internal temperature of 195°F
5. Remove from smoker and let rest for 10 minutes before serving

Nutrition information:
Serving Size: 1 Rib
Calories: 265
Fat: 10g
Carbohydrates: 5g
Protein: 32g
Sodium: 811mg

85. Grilled Chicken Satay Skewers with Peanut Sauce

This grilled chicken satay skewers with peanut sauce is an easy and delicious recipe that will have your guests coming back for more. The dish combines flavorful grilled chicken with a creamy and fragrant peanut sauce for a perfect balance of savory and sweet.
Serving: 4-6
Preparation Time: 10 minutes

Ready Time: 25 minutes

Ingredients:
- 8-10 boneless, skinless chicken thighs
- 2 tablespoons of red curry paste
- 2 tablespoons of vegetable oil
- 2 cloves of garlic, minced
- 2 tablespoons of freshly grated ginger
- 2 tablespoons of honey
- 2 tablespoons of dark soy sauce
- 1 teaspoon of ground coriander
- 1/4 teaspoon of ground turmeric
- 1 cup of unsalted peanut butter
- 1/4 cup of coconut milk
- 2 tablespoons of freshly squeezed lime juice
- 1/4 cup of chopped fresh cilantro
- Salt and pepper to taste

Instructions:
1. Preheat the oven to 375°F.
2. In a medium bowl, combine the red curry paste, vegetable oil, garlic, ginger, honey, soy sauce, coriander and turmeric. Mix until all Ingredients are well blended.
3. Cut the chicken thighs into strips and add to the mixture. Toss until the chicken is evenly coated.
4. Place the chicken skewers on a greased baking sheet and bake in the preheated oven for 15-20 minutes or until the chicken is cooked through.
5. In a separate saucepan, combine the peanut butter, coconut milk, lime juice and cilantro. Simmer on low heat until the sauce is thick and creamy.
6. Serve the chicken skewers with the peanut sauce and enjoy.

Nutrition information: Per Serving: Calories: 467, Protein: 32g, Total Fat: 29g, Total Carbohydrate: 17g, Dietary Fiber: 3g, Sugar: 6g, Vitamin A: 10%, Vitamin C: 10%, Calcium: 5%

86. Smoked Pork Chops with Maple Dijon Glaze

Smoked pork chops with maple Dijon glaze is a delectable classic dish that's surprisingly easy to make at home! A delicious combination of sweet and savory flavors, this is a dish that's sure to be a hit with everyone.
Serving: 4
Preparation time: 10 minutes
Ready time: 20 minutes

Ingredients:
- 4 pork chops
- 2 tablespoons maple syrup
- 1 tablespoon Dijon mustard
- 1 teaspoon garlic powder
- Salt and pepper, to taste
- 2 tablespoons olive oil

Instructions:
1. Preheat the oven to 350 degrees F.
2. Place the pork chops in a baking dish.
3. In a small bowl, combine the maple syrup, Dijon mustard, garlic powder, salt and pepper.
4. Drizzle the mixture over the pork chops, then top with the olive oil.
5. Bake for 20 minutes, or until the pork chops are cooked through.

Nutrition information:
Calories: 276, Protein: 21g, Fat: 15g, Carbohydrates: 7g, Sodium: 394mg, Cholesterol: 72mg

87. Grilled Halloumi and Watermelon Skewers

Grilled Halloumi and Watermelon Skewers are a delicious combination of sweet and salty flavors. These tasty skewers are perfect for summer barbecues or outdoor entertaining.
Serving: 4
Preparation time: 10 minutes
Ready time: 15 minutes

Ingredients:

- 8 ounces of halloumi cheese, cut into cubes
- 2 cups of cubed watermelon
- 8 bamboo skewers
- 2 tablespoons of olive oil
- 2 tablespoons of fresh chopped mint
- Salt and pepper, to taste

Instructions:
1. Preheat the grill to medium-high heat.
2. In a large bowl, combine the halloumi cheese cubes, watermelon cubes, olive oil, chopped mint, salt, and pepper. Mix until all Ingredients are evenly coated.
3. Place two cubes of halloumi and two cubes of watermelon onto each skewer.
4. Grease the grill grate with oil and lay the skewers on the grill.
5. Grill for 5 minutes, flipping the skewers occasionally for even cooking.
6. Serve the skewers warm.

Nutrition information:
Calories: 192 kcal, Carbohydrates: 5 g, Protein: 12 g, Fat: 13 g, Saturated Fat: 7 g, Cholesterol: 35 mg, Sodium: 562 mg, Potassium: 132 mg, Fiber: 0.2 g, Sugar: 4 g, Iron: 0.5 mg.

88. Smoked Bratwurst with Sauerkraut and Mustard

Smoked Bratwurst with Sauerkraut and Mustard is an easy-to-make German classic that is an excellent source of protein and the perfect meal for any occasion.
Serving: 4
Preparation time: 10 minutes
Ready time: 30 minutes

Ingredients:
- 8 smoked bratwurst
- 2 cups of sauerkraut
- 1 tablespoon of olive oil
- 2 teaspoons of Dijon mustard
- 1/2 teaspoon of caraway seeds

• Salt and pepper to taste

Instructions:
1. Pre-heat a large skillet on medium-high heat.
2. Add the olive oil to the skillet and let it heat for a minute.
3. Add the bratwurst to the skillet and cook for about 5 minutes or until golden brown.
4. Add the sauerkraut, caraway seeds, salt and pepper to the skillet and mix everything together.
5. Reduce the heat to low and simmer for 15-20 minutes.
6. Add the mustard and keep stirring until everything is mixed up nicely.
7. Serve with your favorite sides and enjoy!

Nutrition information:
-Calories: 425
-Total Fat: 17 g
-Saturated Fat: 6 g
-Cholesterol: 78 mg
-Sodium: 932 mg
-Carbohydrates: 25 g
-Dietary Fiber: 5 g
-Protein: 33 g

89. Grilled Sweet and Spicy Chicken Wings

These Grilled Sweet and Spicy Chicken Wings are an easy-to-make, flavorful dish that packs a punch. These wings are coated in a delicious sauce made of sweet and spicy Ingredients, and then grilled to perfection.
Serving: This recipe makes 4 servings.
Preparation time: 15 minutes
Ready time
45 minutes

Ingredients:
- 2 lbs chicken wings
- 2 tablespoons olive oil
- 2 tablespoons honey
- 2 tablespoons Sriracha

- 1 teaspoon garlic powder
- ½ teaspoon smoked paprika
- ½ teaspoon onion powder
- Salt and pepper to taste

Instructions:
1. Preheat your grill to 350°F.
2. In a large bowl, toss the wings with the olive oil and season generously with salt and pepper.
3. In a small bowl, whisk together the honey, Sriracha, garlic powder, smoked paprika, and onion powder.
4. Reserve 3 tablespoons of the sauce for basting.
5. Pour the remaining sauce over the wings and toss to coat.
6. Place the wings on the grill and cook for 15 minutes, flipping once, and basting any exposed wings with the reserved sauce.
7. Once the wings are cooked through, remove from the grill and serve warm.

Nutrition information
Serving size: 1/4 of recipe, Calories: 515, Fat: 32g, Saturated fat: 8g, Cholesterol: 146mg, Sodium: 513mg, Carbohydrates: 20g, Sugar: 17g, Protein: 35g

90. Smoked Tri-Tip Sandwiches with Horseradish Sauce

Enjoy a delicious, flavorful sandwich made with smoked tri-tip, lettuce, tomato slices, and a delicious horseradish sauce.
Serving: 4 sandwiches
Preparation Time: 25 minutes
Ready Time: 1 hour

Ingredients:
- 2 lb smoked tri-tip
- 4 sandwich buns
- 2 cups prepared horseradish sauce
- 2 tablespoons fresh parsley, chopped
- 1 cup lettuce, shredded

- 2 tomatoes, sliced

Instructions:
1. Preheat the oven to 400 degrees Fahrenheit.
2. Cut the smoked tri-tip into thin slices. Place the slices on a baking sheet and bake in the preheated oven for 25 minutes.
3. While the tri-tip is baking, toast the sandwich buns.
4. To assemble the sandwiches, spread the horseradish sauce on each sandwich bun. Place thelettuce, tomatoes, and cooked tri-tip on each sandwich bun and top with the other bun. Garnish each sandwich with parsley.

Nutrition information:
- 380 calories
- 25 grams of fat
- 7 grams of saturated fat
- 250 milligrams of cholesterol
- 340 milligrams of sodium
- 22 grams of carbohydrates
- 4 gram of fiber
- 6 grams of sugar
- 33 grams of protein

91. Grilled Vegetable Pasta Salad with Pesto Dressing

Grilled Vegetable Pasta Salad with Pesto Dressing is a fresh and flavorful dish that the whole family can enjoy. This delicious meal is a great way to add more vegetables to your diet and get some delicious flavor.
Serving: Serves 4-6
Preparation Time: 15 minutes
Ready Time: 25 minutes

Ingredients:
- 8 ounces of pasta
- 2 cups of zucchini, diced
- 2 cups of yellow squash, diced
- 1 red bell pepper, diced

- 1/4 cup of olive oil
- 2 cloves garlic, minced
- 1/2 teaspoon of salt
- 1/4 teaspoon of black pepper
- 1/4 cup of pesto
- 1/3 cup of fresh basil, chopped

Instructions:
1. Bring a large pot of salted water to a boil.
2. Add the pasta and cook until al dente.
3. Meanwhile, heat the olive oil in a large skillet over medium heat.
4. Add the zucchini, squash, bell pepper, garlic, salt, and pepper.
5. Cook for 8-10 minutes, stirring occasionally, until vegetables are softened.
6. Drain the pasta and add to the skillet with the vegetables.
7. Add the pesto and basil and stir to combine.
8. Serve the pasta salad warm or chilled.

Nutrition information: 231 calories, 11g fat, 3g saturated fat, 28g carbs, 4g protein, 213mg sodium, 3g sugar, 5g fiber

92. Smoked Chicken Sausage with Peppers and Onions

Smoked chicken sausage makes a delightful meal, especially when combined with sweet peppers and onions. This easy-to-prepare recipe is savory, fragrant, and full of flavor.
Serving: 4
Preparation Time: 10 minutes
Ready Time: 30 minutes

Ingredients:
- 4 smoked chicken sausages (1 ½ lb)
- 2 tablespoons olive oil
- 2 bell peppers (diced)
- 1 large onion (diced)
- ½ teaspoon garlic powder
- ½ teaspoon paprika

- Salt and pepper to taste

Instructions:
1. Heat the olive oil in a large skillet over medium-high heat.
2. Add the sausages to the skillet and cook for 5 minutes, turning occasionally.
3. Add the diced onion and bell peppers and cook for 3 minutes, stirring occasionally.
4. Stir in the garlic powder and paprika and season with salt and pepper.
5. Reduce the heat to medium-low and cook for an additional 15 minutes, stirring occasionally.
6. Serve hot.

Nutrition information:
Calories: 410; Fat: 30g; Carbs: 9g; Protein: 20g; Sodium: 600mg.

93. Grilled Balsamic Glazed Brussels Sprouts

Grilled Balsamic Glazed Brussels Sprouts are a delicious and simple side dish that will add a flavor punch to any meal. This recipe is easy to make and requires minimal Ingredients.
Serving: 4 Servings
Preparation time: 5 minutes
Ready time: 25 minutes

Ingredients:
- 1 pound of brussels sprouts, trimmed and halved
- 2 tablespoons of olive oil
- 2 tablespoons of balsamic vinegar
- 1 teaspoon of garlic powder
- Salt and pepper, to taste

Instructions:
1. Preheat the grill or grill pan to high heat.
2. In a medium bowl, toss the brussels sprouts in olive oil, balsamic vinegar, garlic powder, and salt and pepper.
3. Grill the brussels sprouts cut side down, for 8-10 minutes until the cut sides are charred and the sprouts are tender.

4. Serve the brussels sprouts while warm.

Nutrition information:
Calories: 81 calories, Fat: 5 g, Saturated Fat: 0.8 g, Carbohydrates: 8.7 g, Fiber: 3.7 g, Protein: 3.3 g

94. Smoked Salmon Dip with Dill and Cream Cheese

This Smoked Salmon Dip with Dill and Cream Cheese is a decadent and easy-to-make appetizer or spread that takes advantage of some of the best flavors of Springtime. The combination of sweet smoked salmon, tart cream cheese, and fragrant dill make this dish a mouthwatering delight.
Serving: 4
Preparation Time: 5 minutes
Ready Time: 10 minutes

Ingredients:
- 8 ounces smoked salmon, chopped
- 8 ounces softened cream cheese
- 1/4 cup minced fresh dill
- 2 tablespoons fresh lemon juice
- 1 tablespoon capers
- 1/2 teaspoon black pepper
- Salt to taste

Instructions:
1. In a medium bowl, combine chopped salmon, cream cheese, dill, lemon juice, capers, and pepper.
2. Mix all the Ingredients until fully combined.
3. Season with salt to taste.
4. Cover the bowl and chill in the refrigerator for 10 minutes.
5. Scoop dip onto a plate and serve with crackers or sliced vegetables.

Nutrition information: (per serving)
- Calories: 227
- Fat: 18g
- Carbohydrate: 2g

- Protein: 15g

95. Grilled Tandoori Shrimp Skewers

Grilled Tandoori Shrimp Skewers is a classic Indian-style grilled seafood dish. The skewers are marinated in flavorful tandoori spices then grilled to perfection for a rich, smoky flavor. Serve with flatbreads or a side of basmati rice for a flavorful meal.
Serving: 4
Preparation Time: 30 minutes
Ready Time: 15 minutes

Ingredients:
- 1 pound jumbo shrimp, shelled and deveined
- 2 cloves garlic, minced
- 1 teaspoon fresh ginger, minced
- 2 tablespoons lime juice
- 2 tablespoons Greek yogurt
- 2 tablespoons olive oil
- 1 tablespoon garam masala
- 1/2 teaspoon cumin
- 1/2 teaspoon paprika
- 1/2 teaspoon turmeric
- 1/2 teaspoon ground coriander
- 1/4 teaspoon cayenne pepper
- Salt to taste

Instructions:
1. In a medium bowl, mix together all the Ingredients for the marinade. Add the shrimp and stir to combine. Cover and refrigerate for at least 30 minutes.
2. Once the shrimp is finished marinating, thread the shrimp onto skewers.
3. Preheat your grill to medium-high heat. Grill the shrimp for 2-3 minutes per side, or until cooked through.
4. Serve the grilled shrimp skewers with lime wedges, sliced onion, and cut herbs.

Nutrition information:
Serving Size: 1 skewer
 Calories: 54
 Fat: 3.3 g
 Carbohydrates: 0.9 g
 Protein: 5.2 g

96. Smoked Pork Belly with Honey Soy Glaze

This is a tasty, flavorful dish that combines the smoky flavor of smoked pork belly with a sweet and salty honey soy glaze. The glaze adds a slight crunchiness to the pork, making it a delicious main course or side dish.
Serving: Serves 4
Preparation time: 20 minutes
Ready time: 1 hour

Ingredients:
- 2 lb. smoked pork belly
- 2 tablespoons honey
- 2 tablespoons soy sauce
- 1 teaspoon garlic powder
- 1 teaspoon ground ginger
- 2 tablespoons canola oil

Instructions:
1. Preheat the oven to 375°F (190°C).
2. Cut the smoked pork belly into 4 equal pieces.
3. In a small bowl, mix together the honey, soy sauce, garlic powder, and ground ginger.
4. Place the pork pieces in a baking dish and brush each piece with the honey-soy mixture.
5. Drizzle the canola oil over the pork and rub it in with your fingers.
6. Bake for 40 minutes, basting every 10 minutes with the remaining honey-soy mixture.
7. Once finished, let it rest for 10 minutes before slicing and serving.

Nutrition information: Per serving: 438 calories, 19 g fat, 13 g carbohydrates, 50 g protein.

97. Grilled Portobello Mushroom Burger with Balsamic Reduction

Enjoy the savory flavor of grilled portobello mushrooms and the sweetness of balsamic reduction in this delicious and protein-packed burger!
Serving: 2
Preparation Time: 5 minutes
Ready Time: 20 minutes

Ingredients:
- 2 portobello mushrooms
- 2 burger buns
- 1 tbsp balsamic vinegar
- 2 tsp olive oil
- Salt and pepper to taste
- Optional toppings such as lettuce, tomato, cheese, onion, and pickles

Instructions:
1. Preheat the grill to a medium-high heat.
2. Clean, remove the stem of the portobello mushrooms and season them with the olive oil, salt, and pepper.
3. Place the mushrooms on the heated grill and cook for 4-5 minutes on each side or until the mushrooms are tender.
4. Meanwhile, toast the burger buns if desired.
5. Make the balsamic reduction: Place the balsamic vinegar into a small saucepan and bring it to a boil over medium-high heat. Let it simmer until it thickens and reduce by half.
6. Assemble the burgers: Place a cooked portobello mushroom onto the bottom of each toasted burger bun. Top with your choice of desired toppings and finish it off with a generous drizzle of the balsamic reduction.

Nutrition info:
Calories: 230, Total Fat: 6g, Carbs: 29g, Dietary Fiber: 5g, Protein: 10g

98. Smoked Beef Tenderloin with Blue Cheese Butter

Smoked Beef Tenderloin with Blue Cheese Butter is an incredibly flavorful classic steakhouse dish that's surprisingly easy to make. The blue cheese butter melts over the meat, creating a creamy and delicious crust.

Serving: 2
Preparation time: 15 minutes
Ready Time: 30 minutes

Ingredients:
- 2 (6-ounce) beef tenderloin steaks
- 1 teaspoon dried oregano
- 2 teaspoons smoked paprika
- Salt and freshly ground black pepper to taste
- 1 tablespoon olive oil
- 2 tablespoons butter
- 2 tablespoons blue cheese

Instructions:
1. Rub the steaks with oregano, smoked paprika, and salt and pepper.
2. Heat the olive oil in a large skillet over medium-high heat.
3. Add the steaks and cook for 5 minutes per side for medium-rare, or until desired doneness is achieved.
4. Remove the steaks from the skillet and set aside.
5. In the same skillet, reduce the heat to low and add the butter.
6. Once the butter has completely melted, stir in the blue cheese.
7. Return the steaks to the skillet and baste them with the blue cheese butter.
8. Cook for an additional 1-2 minutes, or until the blue cheese butter is melted and the steak is cooked through.

Nutrition information:
Calories: 290, Fat: 14.9g, Saturated Fat: 6.2g, Carbohydrates: 0.5g, Protein: 36.0g, Sodium: 312.9mg

99. Grilled Pineapple Upside-Down Cake

Grilled Pineapple Upside-Down Cake is a delicious and unique dessert made with pineapple rings, brown sugar, and cake batter. It's perfect to enjoy on its own or paired with a scoop of ice cream.
Serving: 8-10
Preparation Time: 10 minutes
Ready Time: 25 minutes

Ingredients:
-3 tablespoons of butter, melted
-1/3 cup packed brown sugar
-4-5 pineapple rings, canned or fresh
-1/2 cup chopped pecans
-1 (18.25 ounce) package yellow cake mix
-1/4 cup butter, melted

Instructions:
1. Preheat grill to 350 degrees F (175 degrees C).
2. Mix melted butter and brown sugar and spread mixture onto a piece of heavy-duty aluminum foil, large enough to fit all of the pineapple rings.
3. Arrange the pineapple rings in a single layer on top of the brown sugar mixture. Sprinkle the pecans over the pineapple rings.
4. Prepare the cake mix according to the instructions on the package and pour the batter on top of the pineapple rings.
5. Dot the top of the cake with butter.
6. Place the foil on the grill, cover, and cook for 25-30 minutes.
7. Remove from the grill and serve the cake warm or cold.

Nutrition information: Per Serving: 401 calories; 16.2 g fat; 67.2 g carbohydrates; 4.4 g protein; 94 mg cholesterol; 402 mg sodium.

100. Smoked Apple Crisp with Vanilla Ice Cream

Smoked Apple Crisp with Vanilla Ice Cream is an irresistible treat. This classic dessert combines smoky apples with a crispy oat crumble topping and is served with creamy vanilla ice cream. It's a delicious way to end a meal and a great way to get everyone together for an after-dinner treat.

Serving:
Makes 8 servings
Preparation Time: 10 minutes
Ready Time: 50 minutes

Ingredients:
- 4 medium Granny Smith apples, peeled, cored, and sliced into 1/4 inch thick slices
- 2 tablespoons extra-virgin olive oil
- 2 teaspoons smoked paprika
- 1 teaspoon ground cinnamon
- 1/2 teaspoon ground nutmeg
- 1/4 teaspoon fine sea salt
- 2 cups rolled oats
- 1/2 cup packed light brown sugar
- 1/2 cup melted butter
- 1/2 teaspoon vanilla extract
- Vanilla ice cream, for Serving:

Instructions:
1. Preheat oven to 375°F (190°C).
2. In a large bowl, toss the sliced apples with the olive oil, smoked paprika, cinnamon, nutmeg, and sea salt.
3. Spread the apples into an 8-inch baking dish.
4. In a separate bowl, mix together the rolled oats, brown sugar, melted butter, and vanilla extract until crumbly.
5. Sprinkle the oat mixture evenly over the apples.
6. Bake for 40 minutes or until the top is golden brown and crisp.
7. Let cool slightly before serving with vanilla ice cream.

Nutrition information:
Calories: 250; Total fat: 11g; Saturated fat: 6g; Trans fat: 0g; Cholesterol: 20mg; Sodium: 80mg; Carbohydrates: 36g; Dietary Fiber: 4g; Sugars: 16g; Protein: 3g

101. Grilled Banana Splits with Chocolate Sauce

This dish provides a unique way to combine the decadent flavors of banana and chocolate in a classic dessert with a twist. Grilled banana splits with chocolate sauce are a fun and delicious treat suitable for any occasion.

Serving: 4
Preparation Time: 10 minutes
Ready Time: 25 minutes

Ingredients:
- 4 large bananas
- 2 tablespoons of olive oil
- 4 scoops of ice cream or frozen yogurt
- 1/2 cup of dark chocolate chips
- 3 tablespoons of butter
- 2 tablespoons of sugar
- 1/2 cup of heavy cream
- Sliced almonds and whipped cream for garnish

Instructions:
1. Preheat the grill to high heat.
2. Cut each banana in half lengthwise and drizzle with olive oil.
3. Place the banana halves on the grill and cook for about 8-10 minutes, flipping once.
4. Meanwhile, melt the chocolate chips, butter and sugar in a double boiler or in the microwave.
5. Remove the grilled banana halves and top each one with a scoop of ice cream or frozen yogurt.
6. Pour the chocolate sauce over the banana splits.
7. Garnish with sliced almonds and whipped cream and enjoy.

Nutrition information:
Calories: 340, Total Fat: 19g, Saturated Fat: 11g, Cholesterol: 45mg, Sodium: 95mg, Carbohydrates: 45g, Fiber: 4g, Sugar: 31g, Protein: 3g

CONCLUSION

"Green Egg Extravaganza: 101 Recipes for Grilling and Smoking with the Big Green Egg"

As we come to the end of our journey through "Green Egg Extravaganza: 101 Recipes for Grilling and Smoking with the Big Green Egg," we find ourselves immersed in the smoky aroma, bold flavors, and culinary excitement that grilling and smoking on the Big Green Egg brings. This extraordinary cookbook has taken us on a grilling adventure, offering 101 recipes that showcase the versatility and exceptional results that can be achieved with this iconic cooking vessel.

Throughout this cookbook, we have explored the art of grilling and smoking on the Big Green Egg—a culinary experience like no other. From perfectly seared steaks and succulent ribs to tender vegetables and smoky-infused desserts, each recipe has been crafted to highlight the capabilities of the Big Green Egg and inspire us to elevate our outdoor cooking skills.

What sets "Green Egg Extravaganza" apart is its dedication to the art of grilling and smoking. It celebrates the traditions of outdoor cooking while embracing innovation and creativity. Whether you're a seasoned grill master or a novice, this cookbook provides a comprehensive guide to mastering the techniques, exploring new flavors, and pushing the boundaries of what can be achieved with the Big Green Egg.

With 101 recipes at our disposal, we have been introduced to a diverse range of grilling and smoking possibilities. From classic favorites to innovative creations, each recipe invites us to embark on a culinary adventure and discover the unique flavor profiles that can be achieved on the Big Green Egg. Whether it's a perfectly grilled whole chicken, a melt-in-your-mouth rack of ribs, a smoky and tender pulled pork, or a flavorful grilled vegetable medley, these recipes inspire us to unleash our creativity and make every outdoor cooking experience a memorable one.

Beyond the sheer pleasure of grilling and smoking, "Green Egg Extravaganza" recognizes the importance of gathering and celebrating with loved ones. It reminds us that cooking on the Big Green Egg is not just about the food—it's about creating memorable moments, forging connections, and sharing the joys of outdoor cooking with family and friends. The Big Green Egg becomes the centerpiece of gatherings, a catalyst for togetherness, and a source of warmth and celebration.

As we conclude this grilling extravaganza, it is important to remember that "Green Egg Extravaganza" is more than just a cookbook—it is an invitation to embrace the outdoor cooking experience, to connect with the primal instincts of fire and smoke, and to revel in the joy of creating flavorful, unforgettable meals. It encourages us to venture outside, breathe in the fresh air, and immerse ourselves in the sensory delights of grilling and smoking on the Big Green Egg.

So, as we bid farewell to "Green Egg Extravaganza," let us carry the knowledge, inspiration, and excitement we have gained throughout this culinary journey. May the 101 recipes continue to ignite our passion for grilling and smoking, encourage us to explore new flavors and techniques, and create extraordinary meals that leave a lasting impression. Let us embrace the smoky aromas, the sizzling sounds, and the mouthwatering flavors that can be achieved on the Big Green Egg.

Here's to the art of grilling and smoking, the thrill of outdoor cooking, and the shared moments of joy around the grill. With "Green Egg Extravaganza" as our guide, may our future grilling endeavors be filled with delicious flavors, cherished memories, and the camaraderie that comes with sharing exceptional meals with our loved ones. Let us continue to embrace the power of fire and smoke, elevate our outdoor cooking skills, and savor the flavors that can only be achieved on the Big Green Egg.

Milton Keynes UK
Ingram Content Group UK Ltd.
UKHW021824101023
430294UK00020B/693